CLEVELAND STATE UNIVERSITY: 50 YEARS

Proud Past, Unlimited Future

Regennia N. Williams, Ph.D.

Edited by John Soeder

Williams, Regennia N. *Cleveland State University: 50 Years.* Cleveland, Ohio: MSL Academic Endeavors, 2014.
Cleveland State University – History
Universities and colleges – Ohio – Cleveland – History

ISBN-10: 0-692-27498-7
ISBN-13: 978-0-692-27498-9

For Brian, Horace and Timothy

Acknowledgments

Grateful acknowledgment is hereby given to the following:

Cleveland State University 50th Anniversary Committee

Dr. Julian Earls, Chair

Dr. Ronald M. Berkman, President
and
Dr. Michael Schwartz, President Emeritus,
Co-Chairs

The Michael Schwartz Library, Cleveland State University

William Barrow, Special Collections
William Becker, University Archives
Lynn Duchez Bycko, Special Collections
Barbara Strauss, Assistant Director

University Marketing

Kate Circelli
Lisa Doyle
Julie Goulis
Jennifer Moran
David Roll
John Soeder
Rob Spademan
Kevin Ziegler

Dr. Deirdre Mageean, Provost and Senior Vice President for Academic Affairs

and

Dr. Ralph Kidder, Dr. Leonard Moore, Dr. Dennis Keating, Barbara Chudzik and other readers

Photos from the Cleveland State University Archives

CONTENTS

Letter from Governor John R. Kasich   vii

Letter from Mayor Frank G. Jackson   ix

Letter from CSU 50th Anniversary Committee   xi

Foreword: "An Excellent Suggestion"   1

President Harold Enarson 1966-1972   4

President Walter Waetjen 1973-1988   22

President John Flower 1988-1992   38

President Claire Van Ummersen 1993-2001   50

President Michael Schwartz 2001-2009   60

President Ronald M. Berkman 2009-Present   76

Afterword: "Here, There, Everywhere Vikings!"   92

A Note from the Author   94

JOHN R. KASICH
GOVERNOR
STATE OF OHIO

On behalf of the State of Ohio, we congratulate Cleveland State University on the commemoration of 50 years of quality higher education in the City of Cleveland.

Cleveland State's founding in 1964 marked a significant change in Northeast Ohio higher education. In the 1960s, James Rhodes, then candidate for governor, promised that every Ohio citizen would have access to a college within 30 miles of their home. On December 18, 1964, Governor Rhodes signed Ohio General Assembly Amended House Bill No. 2 creating Cleveland State and opened a door to opportunity for residents of Cleveland's urban neighborhoods who had previously lacked access to a four-year public college.

Fifty years later, as one of 14 universities in the University System of Ohio, Cleveland State is essential to ensuring that Northeast Ohioans have access to a high-quality, affordable education. The University's innovative efforts to promote students' success serve as a national example for increasing college completion. These efforts are preparing students to graduate and serve the region's critical workforce needs. Cleveland State is one of Cleveland's strongest resources and is essential to sustaining the city's economic vitality.

The State of Ohio is proud to recognize all that this institution has achieved in its first 50 years. This is just the beginning of what will be an enduring tradition of educational excellence at Cleveland State.

Sincerely,

John R. Kasich
Governor, State of Ohio

CITY OF CLEVELAND
Mayor Frank G. Jackson

For 50 years, Cleveland State University has served as a center of access to higher education and opportunity for the citizens of Cleveland.

Cleveland State is also my alma mater. The University gave me the chance to achieve my academic goals. I earned my bachelor's and master's degrees from the University and worked as a night clerk for the Cleveland Municipal Court to put myself through Cleveland-Marshall College of Law. Cleveland State provided a pathway for me to succeed and pursue a meaningful career, just as it has done for more than 100,000 alumni.

The University is uniquely committed to preparing students for a successful career post-graduation. Today's Cleveland State students are tomorrow's urban physicians and lawyers. They are our public servants and educators; our business leaders and residential developers. I am confident knowing that future generations of Cleveland State students will continue to fuel our city's workforce.

Cleveland State has set an example of engaged partnership in the City of Cleveland and strengthens our communities through its investment and collaboration. In particular, the University's efforts with the Cleveland Metropolitan School District will better educate the children of our city and ensure that more young people fulfill their dream of going to college.

Congratulations to the University on a significant legacy and impact in Cleveland which will only continue to grow.

Sincerely,

Frank G. Jackson
Mayor, City of Cleveland
Bachelor of Arts, 1977
Master of Science, 1979
Juris Doctorate, 1983

On the sunny afternoon of September 19, 2014, thousands of students, faculty, staff, alumni and friends descended on Euclid Avenue and East 18th Street downtown for a grand celebration in honor of our University's 50th anniversary. There were well-known entertainers and musicians, foods from favorite Cleveland establishments and a vibrant fireworks display. But what was most memorable about the occasion was the profound sense of connection between Cleveland State and the community we serve.

Our University's founding mission was to offer an exceptional and accessible education to the people of Cleveland. The creation of Cleveland State filled a critical void for those residents of Cleveland's urban communities who did not have access to a four-year public institution.

Cleveland State, built upon the rich tradition of our predecessor, Fenn College, became Ohio's seventh state university. Since the first classes were held in the fall of 1965, the University has provided a critical educational opportunity to those in our region seeking a college degree. Today, Cleveland State is a destination for talented, academically strong students desiring a world-class education.

In early 2013, we convened a committee comprised of individuals across the University and community to help commemorate our 50th anniversary year. Students, faculty, community leaders and Board of Trustees members alike joined together to plan all the elements of this singular milestone, including the creation of this book.

Cleveland State University: 50 Years is a testament to our journey and how far we have come. It documents our rich history, in which we take great pride, and reminds us of unique moments in our past. We anticipate many more milestones in the life of this extraordinary University. As we celebrate, we want to recognize the wonderful, diverse group of students, faculty, staff, alumni and friends who together will define the future of Cleveland State University.

Sincerely,

Dr. Julian Earls
Chair, Cleveland State University
50th Anniversary Committee

President Ronald M. Berkman
Honorary Co-Chair

President Emeritus
Michael Schwartz
Honorary Co-Chair

"An Excellent Suggestion"

A UNIVERSITY GROWS IN CLEVELAND

When plans were being laid for a public university in Cleveland, American people of all ages were on the move for change.

Hundreds of thousands of people had marched on Washington, D.C., for "Jobs and Freedom." Students at the University of California at Berkeley marched in defense of free speech. Other activists organized and marched for civil rights, voting rights and women's rights, among other causes. Even as the federal government launched the Great Society programs, Americans were marching off to war in Southeast Asia in growing numbers, and many college students were joining forces with others to march in opposition to – or in support of – the nation's growing involvement in the Vietnam War.

In the midst of a decade when the times were a-changin', as Bob Dylan sang, one year in particular was especially eventful. U.S. space probe Ranger 7 beamed the first close-up images of the Moon back to Earth. Closer to home, a rock 'n' roll quartet from Liverpool, England, called the Beatles took America by storm and the Cleveland Browns won the NFL championship.

The year was 1964 – and it also witnessed the birth of Cleveland State University. Or "The Cleveland State University," as it was often referred to in the beginning.

During his election campaign two years earlier, Ohio Governor James Rhodes had proposed that there should be a state university within a 30-mile radius of every Ohio resident. At that time, Kent State University was the nearest state university to Cleveland.

In the meantime, Fenn College was struggling. The administration of the private institution called upon the State of Ohio to develop a state university in Cleveland, with Fenn College as its nucleus.

When classes began in 1965, CSU comprised only three buildings – surrounded by a sea of parking lots.

In a letter dated July 3, 1964, from Rhodes to Harold Oyster, chairman of the Ohio Board of Regents, Rhodes wrote:

This is a formal acknowledgment of receipt of your letter of June 24 in which, as Chairman of the Ohio Board of Regents, you transmitted the recommendation of the Board that action be taken by the Ohio General Assembly to establish by law a new state university to be located in Cleveland and to be named the "Cleveland State University."

Rhodes went on to praise the recommendation as "an excellent suggestion."

The Ohio General Assembly approved the measure – Amended House Bill No. 2 – on December 17, 1964. The following day, with a stroke of his pen, Rhodes signed the bill into law and created Ohio's seventh state university: Cleveland State University.

Fast-forward 50 years. Located in the heart of the city, CSU is the academic home of more than 17,000 students and 2,000 faculty and staff. These totals are a far cry from the fall of 1965, the first official term for CSU, when there were fewer than 5,600 full-time and part-time students and fewer than 250 faculty members. Back then, men outnumbered women in the student body three to one, and the physical plant included just three buildings.

Today, with an 85-acre campus, CSU casts the largest footprint of any downtown Cleveland institution. Its growth and expansion are contributing to the ongoing renaissance in neighboring PlayhouseSquare and all along the city's Euclid Corridor.

The University's endowment is valued at $72.3 million, with student scholarships representing more than half of that amount. This is especially noteworthy when one considers that there was no endowment at the time of the school's founding.

In 2014, CSU could look back on the first half century of its history and point with pride to the fact that it had produced more than 120,000 alumni, most of whom continued to live and work in Northeast Ohio after graduation. In addition to contributing to the transformation of life on America's North Coast, CSU alumni were also living and working throughout the United States and 60 other countries across the globe.

At the same time, many things about CSU have not changed. Dedicated faculty members have always been crucial to the institution's success in the areas of classroom teaching, student learning, research and creative activities. Cultural and intellectual diversity continue to be top priorities, and signature programs bring some of the world's top scholars and artists to campus. Throughout the University's history, a dynamic campus life also has been important. Extracurricular and co-curricular activities have long involved events hosted by fraternities, sororities and other student organizations, fine and performing arts events and exciting athletic programs.

No book of this size could present a comprehensive history of Cleveland's public university. This brief illustrated history seeks instead to shed new light on some of the University's major accomplishments and greatest challenges since 1964. The hope is that this volume will present a balanced account of the institution's past.

CSU's history was shaped in no small measure by the forces that challenged all American institutions of higher learning and the wider society in the second half of the 20th century and the beginning of the 21st century. In the final analysis, it must be noted that, despite pressure from internal and external forces, the University remains strong, energized by a determination to learn from its past, while playing a vital role in shaping post-secondary education in the future.

President

HAROLD ENARSON

1966-72

"So Much...in So Little Time"

Cleveland State University came into being seemingly overnight. But its backstory spanned nearly a century.

The University's origins can be traced to 1870, when the Cleveland Young Men's Christian Association launched an educational program offering free night classes in German and French. Four day schools opened in the early 1900s, which eventually led to the establishment of the Cleveland YMCA School of Technology, aka "Y-Tech."

The latter institution was reborn as Fenn College in 1930, named after Sereno Peck Fenn, president of the Cleveland YMCA for 25 years. (Lore has it that graduates had yearned for something more prestigious-sounding than "YMCA" on their diplomas.)

Adopting a pioneering cooperative education program that alternated classroom studies with practical workplace experience, Fenn College weathered the trying economic times of the Great Depression, which dominated the first decade of its history. Seeking more space for classrooms and offices, the college purchased the National Town and Country Club skyscraper on the corner of Euclid Avenue and East 24th Street in 1937. One year later, it was dedicated as Fenn Tower.

Fenn College played a significant role as a provider of war-training programs during World War II, which brought much-needed financial support and thousands of special students to Fenn, including, beginning in February 1943, those in the fledgling U.S. Army Air Corps program. Many who had been degree-seeking students and faculty members at Fenn at the outset of the war would also be counted among those who served, were captured as prisoners of war or declared missing in action, or died during the hostilities. Government support in the form of the G.I. Bill led many returning veterans to enroll in the post-war era.

By the early 1960s, Fenn faced mounting challenges, including increased operating costs, direct competition from the new Cuyahoga Community College and whispers of a possible state takeover. In "The Fenn Plan for Unified Public Higher Education in Cleveland-Northeastern Ohio," prepared in 1963, the college stated that its "plan of action [would] aid in resolving the effective and efficient coordination of public higher education in Northeastern Ohio so that education opportunities will be available to all." Historian Ralph Kidder pointed out that the 1963 plan was, in essence, "about how to position Fenn College so that it could be sold to the State of Ohio."

When the Ohio General Assembly created Cleveland State University and passed Amended House Bill No. 2 on December 17, 1964, it did so with the support of administrators at Fenn College, as well as Governor James Rhodes and a host of other business, civic, educational, industrial and political leaders. Rhodes was the foremost proponent of the plan to build a state university in Cleveland, the nation's eighth largest city and the most populous in the state of Ohio, with 876,050 residents in 1960.

After signing the House Bill into law, Rhodes quickly appointed nine men to the CSU Board of Trustees. Less than a week later, on December 22, 1964, they held their first informal meeting and began sorting out the details of the agreement that would transfer Fenn College to state control.

The CSU Board of Trustees held its first official meeting at the Hotel Statler on January 5, 1965. Clockwise from left are Joseph Bartunek, Abe Silverstein, Ernest Johnson, Edward Sloan Jr., Warren Chase, James Nance, Curtis Lee Smith, William Taft and Middleton Lambright.

Dr. Harry Newburn was named acting president of CSU in August 1965. Prior to his appointment, he served as an educational consultant for the University's academic master plan.

Time was of the essence. "We know something must be done in a hurry, but it has to be done right," said CSU Trustee William Taft, a state representative.

The University welcomed its first class of undergraduates on September 28, 1965. Only six months earlier, the final acceptance of the agreement between the University and Fenn College had arranged for the transfer of Fenn's land, buildings, equipment, staff and faculty to CSU. Fewer than seven weeks before classes began, Dr. Harry Newburn, a professor of education from the University of Arizona who had served as a special consultant to the transition committee, was appointed acting president of CSU, even as the Board of Trustees quickly sought to fill the top spot permanently with an individual who possessed "political acumen, physical stamina and an imaginative temperament."

Soon enough, they had their man: Dr. Harold Enarson.

CSU's first president couldn't help but marvel at the instantaneousness of it all. "New colleges and universities are being created throughout the land," Dr. Enarson observed shortly after he took office at CSU on February 1, 1966. "But is there another city where so much has been done in so little time?"

Dr. Enarson was born in Iowa and raised in New Mexico. After graduating with honors from the University of New Mexico, he enlisted in the U.S. Army immediately following Pearl Harbor. He went on to earn a master's degree from Stanford University and a doctorate in political science and public administration from American University in Washington, D.C.

Dr. Enarson was known for his iconic pipe.

Modular buildings provided additional classroom and office space. Leased from the Modulux Corporation of California in 1967, the temporary structures stood until 1972 on the present-day site of the Physical Education Building.

Prior to coming to CSU, he served as administrative vice president at the University of New Mexico and as executive director of the Western Interstate Commission for Higher Education. Between puffs on his ever-present tobacco pipe, he would joke about moving to Cleveland with only one regret: having to leave two horses behind in Albuquerque.

Decisiveness was his strong suit, although it may have manifested itself most dramatically *after* Dr. Enarson left CSU to assume the presidency of The Ohio State University. There, he would become famous (infamous?) for firing Woody Hayes after the legendary Buckeyes football coach punched a player on the opposing team when OSU lost to Alabama in the 1978 Gator Bowl.

Bold, swift strokes also characterized Dr. Enarson's leadership at CSU. It was a period of tremendous growth across the University, complete with new buildings on a rapidly expanding campus (from nine acres to 27 acres) that was coming into its own, the formation of numerous academic programs and exponential growth in enrollment.

At times, the University struggled to keep pace. To meet constant demand for more classroom space and more office space, the Board of Trustees leased seven modular buildings from the Modulux Corporation of California in 1967. Students, faculty and staff made do with these temporary facilities, located just north of Fenn Tower, until 1972.

In the interim, cranes and construction crews were familiar sights, building the first phase of a campus master plan unveiled in April 1966. Its emphasis on modernistic architecture inspired wisecracks about "Concrete State University" and met with disapproval from at least one prominent critic. "This is not what I think an urban university should look like," said Cleveland Museum of Art Director Sherman Lee, a member of Cleveland's Fine Arts Advisory Committee. He decried the campus plan as "inhuman" and "like a machine." With a green light from the City Planning Commission, though, Cleveland's urban university started taking shape.

In November 1966, a groundbreaking ceremony was held for the first new addition to campus: the Science Building. Plans called for a limestone and brick structure with classrooms and laboratories for biology, chemistry and physics, topped with a cantilevered fourth floor. It opened in the fall of 1969 on the northwest corner of Euclid Avenue and East 24th Street.

Two years later, University Tower and the Main Classroom Building were feted with a joint dedication ceremony on October 20, 1971.

Staking CSU's claim in Cleveland's skyline, University Tower rose 21 stories above the city. The limestone skyscraper housed hundreds of faculty offices, audio-visual facilities and computer labs, as well as a new library with space for 450,000 volumes and seating for 2,000 students.

Left: CSU celebrated the groundbreaking for the Science Building with a luncheon at the Hotel Sheraton-Cleveland. From left are Dr. Harold Enarson, Cleveland Mayor Ralph Locher, Ohio Governor James Rhodes and CSU Board of Trustees Chair James Nance.

Above: The first building constructed for CSU was the Science Building, on the northwest corner of Euclid Avenue and East 24th Street. It opened in the fall of 1969.

The Main Classroom Building, which had been in use for a year prior to its formal dedication, boasted 56 classrooms, 22 laboratories, a 478-seat auditorium, lounges, study rooms and an underground parking garage. It laid claim to being the largest classroom building in Ohio.

CSU desperately needed the additional space. By the fall of 1970, the University had an enrollment of 11,100 students. This was more than three times the fall 1965 figure of 3,375. Since then, the number of full-time faculty had nearly tripled, from 145 to 406, and a total of 3,980 degrees had been awarded.

In 1967, the University Bookstore moved from the first floor of Fenn Tower across Euclid Avenue to a new location in the rear of the Bell Motors building.

The need for additional space led the University Library to open an Undergraduate Library in the front section of the Bell Motors building, which also housed the University Bookstore. Pictured from left are Dr. Joseph Ink, professor of history, and Dr. Major Jenks, dean of the College of Arts and Sciences.

"From the beginning, there has rarely been enough of anything – enough course options, enough cafeteria facilities, enough books and seats in the library, enough recreational space and – you guessed it – enough parking spaces," Dr. Enarson said. "It is as if we were perpetual migrants in the perennial search and scrimp for expanded space. For this I make no apology. Inconvenience is a small price to pay when the alternative is the denial of opportunity to the young people who want to live in Cleveland and go to CSU."

From the earliest days of the University's history, accessibility and affordability were top priorities. While there was no endowment fund to speak of, CSU offered scholarships as well as fee waivers by 1966.

CSU held its first commencement on June 12, 1966, at the Masonic Auditorium in Cleveland. The first degree was conferred upon Maggie Allen, a transfer student who majored in social work.

CSU's first commencement was held on June 12, 1966, in Masonic Auditorium. New York University President James Hester delivered the address.

From Fenn College, CSU inherited its three original colleges: the College of Engineering, the College of Business and the College of Arts and Sciences. In 1966, the College of Education was established. The following year, CSU added graduate degree programs (starting with engineering and mathematics), which led to the establishment of the College of Graduate Studies in 1968. Doctoral degree programs were implemented one year later.

By the end of the decade, CSU had added a sixth college: the Cleveland-Marshall College of Law. Its roots went back to the Cleveland Law School, founded in 1897, the first evening law school in Ohio and the first to admit women. It merged with the John Marshall School of Law in 1946. The subsequent merger between CSU and Cleveland-Marshall was finalized on June 25, 1969.

 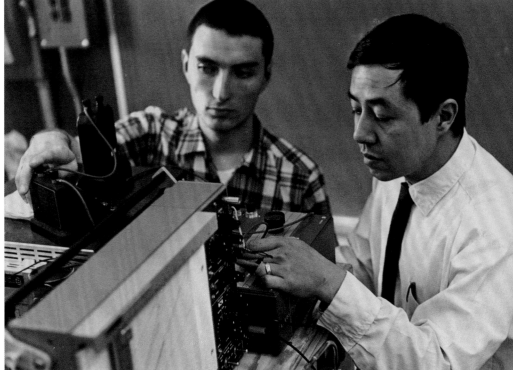

Left: The College of Education was established in 1966. From left are founding faculty members Dr. Floyd Adams, Lucille Ringel, Dr. Gordon Samson, Dr. Richard McArdle and Dr. Murray Schneider.

Right: One of the earliest graduate degree programs offered was the master of science in physics, established in 1969. At right is Steiner Huang, associate professor of physics at CSU from 1964 to 1988.

University and community officials gathered at the Cuyahoga County Courthouse on June 25, 1969, to sign a merger agreement between CSU and the Cleveland-Marshall Law School. From left are Dr. Harold Enarson; CSU Trustee James Nance; Cleveland-Marshall Trustees Dwight Buss and Carl Wasmuth; Cleveland-Marshall Dean James Gaynor; and Common Pleas Court Chief Justice John Corrigan.

For a young institution, CSU also made impressive strides in scholarly activity and faculty research – despite the fact that Dr. Enarson had told *The Cauldron:* "We are not trying to be Harvard on the Cuyahoga." Dr. Louis Millic of the Department of English published "A Quantitative Approach to the Style of Jonathan Swift," one of the first humanities studies to utilize computer analysis. Dr. Herman Meisner of the Department of Biology conducted research on cancer and the heart, sup-

ported by grants from the National Institutes of Health, the Heart Association of Northeastern Ohio and the Cleveland Health Fund. And a study by Dr. Robert Rolan of CSU's Institute for Urban Studies (precursor to the Maxine Goodman Levin College of Urban Affairs) was credited with providing evidence to scuttle a proposal (originally suggested by Cleveland Mayor Ralph Locher) to build a large airport on an artificial island in the middle of Lake Erie.

Student life blossomed on the burgeoning campus, too. Ohio State Representative Carl Stokes (a Cleveland-Marshall College of Law alumnus who later became mayor of Cleveland) was grand marshal of the parade for CSU's first Homecoming on November 6, 1965. The festivities also included a formal dance in Fenn Tower.

In the fall of 1970, one floor of dormitory rooms in Fenn Tower – which had been home to approximately 200 male students – was opened for female students. Peggy Polley, associate dean of student life, told *The Plain Dealer* that the co-ed dorm was an "experiment" and said that the women would be expected to live under the same rules as the men. Apparently, the experiment was a success – three years later, the housing policy was revised to allow women and men to reside on the same floors.

The University's first Student Center opened in 1972 in the McKee Building on Euclid Avenue, which would be torn down seven years later to make way for the Science and Research Building. The unofficial student center was Fat Glenn's, a rathskeller in the basement of Mather Mansion (which CSU purchased from the Cleveland Automobile Club in 1970). In this cozy hideaway beneath the last of the palatial homes built along Euclid Avenue's "Millionaire's Row," 3.2 beer was the beverage of choice and the entertainment ranged from local bands to internationally renowned artist Peter Max, who held a "rap session" there in January 1972. Named after Glenn Esch, assistant to CSU's dean of student life, Fat Glenn's remained a popular campus hangout for two decades.

CSU held its first Homecoming on November 6, 1965. Grand Marshal Carl Stokes, future mayor of Cleveland, led a parade that started downtown and traveled up Euclid Avenue to Fenn Tower.

Students relax by the fountain on the front lawn of Mather Mansion. The last of the mansions built along "Millionaire's Row," it was constructed by shipping magnate Samuel Mather and completed in 1910. Sixty years later, CSU purchased the mansion from the Cleveland Automobile Club.

The CSU Inaugural Ball and Fenn College Alumni Homecoming drew an 1,800-strong crowd to the Hotel Sheraton-Cleveland on December 3, 1965. Musical entertainment was provided by singer Dionne Warwick, who performed with the Billy Lang Orchestra.

John McLendon, left, coached basketball at CSU from 1966 to 1969. At right is James Rodriguez, assistant basketball coach.

Like the rest of the University, CSU's athletics program got off to a very quick start – so quick, in fact, that when the soccer team played its first intercollegiate match in September 1965, the University had yet to settle on a nickname for its athletic squads. (The anonymous team won anyway, 3-0.) One month later, students voted in favor of "Vikings" in a contest sponsored by *The Cleveland Press.*

Longtime Fenn College Athletic Director Homer Woodling, who also coached baseball, basketball, track and other sports at the college, served as CSU's first athletic director. He was succeeded in 1966 by Robert Busbey, who held the post for 24 years and built a solid athletics program with 18 intercollegiate sports for men and women.

Early on, the men's basketball team was coached by Basketball Hall of Famer John McLendon, a leading proponent of the fast break and a trailblazer who broke racial barriers. He learned basketball straight from the man who invented the game: Dr. James Naismith. After three straight championship seasons at Tennessee State University, McLendon became the first black head coach of a pro basketball team when he led the American Basketball League's Cleveland Pipers (owned by George Steinbrenner) during the 1961-1962 season. In 1966, McLendon came to CSU, where he was the first black basketball coach at a predominantly white university. Following three seasons (which included his 500th career victory), he left to coach the Denver Rockets in the American Basketball Association. After retiring from coaching, he returned to CSU in the 1990s to serve as an Athletics Department advisor.

Dr. Thomas Campbell, left, founded the CSU Institute of Urban Affairs. In May 1967, Dr. Campbell and Dr. Albert Cousins, right, held an anti-poverty summit at CSU. They're shown here speaking with U.S. Representative Jerry Voorhees of California.

As CSU was coming together, there were times when its hometown appeared to be coming apart at the seams.

In July 1966, race riots erupted in the Hough neighborhood on Cleveland's East Side, not quite three miles from campus. Amid the vandalism, looting, arson and gunfire, four people were killed, 30 people were injured and nearly 300 arrests were made. The National Guard was called in to restore order.

This type of urban unrest became the subject of an oft-quoted 1968 report published by the National Advisory Commission on Civil Disorders. There is

evidence to suggest that many CSU students, faculty and staff were willing to address the concerns expressed in this report and related documents.

More than a year earlier, Professor Albert Cousins had forwarded to Dr. Enarson a report titled "A Society's Need: A University's Duty" that outlined a social service curriculum at CSU. Professors Cousins, Mareyjoyce Green and Butler Jones of the University's sociology department helped to lay the foundation for what would become the School of Social Work and the Women's Comprehensive Program.

Also during this era, in response to concerns expressed by black student activists, faculty and staff, CSU launched a Black Studies Program in 1969, followed in short order by an Afro-American Cultural Center and *The Vindicator,* a multicultural student publication.

In June 1969, Cleveland made national headlines when the Cuyahoga River – or, more accurately, oily debris floating on the surface of the extremely polluted river – caught fire. Courtesy of "Laugh-In" and other comedians, Cleveland soon became the butt of countless jokes. "The Mistake on the Lake," some called it.

Cleveland had more to lose than pride; it was losing population and jobs, too, as deindustrialization accelerated. Its public school system was in decline, crime was increasing and urban blight was setting in.

Speaking before the City Club of Cleveland on June 23, 1972, only weeks before his departure for The Ohio State University, Dr. Enarson reiterated CSU's commitment to Cleveland.

Top: Cleveland firefighters were called to the scene when a group of black CSU students burned copies of the June 4, 1969, edition of *The Cauldron* to protest a controversial editorial cartoon. The incident was one of several events that led to the creation of CSU's Black Studies Program and a multicultural student publication, *The Vindicator.*

Bottom: The Afro-American Cultural Center opened in Mather Mansion in 1970. Four years later, it moved to University Center. The center was renamed in 2004 in honor of Dr. Howard Mims, longtime director of CSU's Black Studies Program.

Congressman Louis Stokes, seated at left, and Cleveland Mayor Carl Stokes, center, joined Dr. Enarson outside Mather Mansion on October 28, 1970, at the dedication ceremonies for the Afro-American Cultural Center.

"We have discovered that only as we sharpen our role as a university are we able to serve the community," he said. "Our urban contributions are the new programs such as the third- and fourth-year program in engineering technology, the master's-level programs in business and education, health sciences programs, the new master's program in urban studies, the Black Studies Program and the special assistance given the academically disadvantaged. These and other programs are in tune with the needs of the day."

Saving the day would prove to be a much taller order in the years ahead.

President

WALTER WAETJEN

1973-88

"Made to Order"

An urban university best serves its city by best serving its students. This was the philosophy of Cleveland State University's second president, Dr. Walter Waetjen.

"An urban university can involve itself in certain aspects of the community, but only for the purpose of educating students," he said in an address before the City Club of Cleveland on November 7, 1975. "This is the role given us by the state."

Dr. Waetjen was CSU's longest-serving president, holding the office for 15 years. His tenure marked a period of maturation, with CSU seeking to define its role as an urban university. While the campus continued to grow and enrollment continued to climb, academic, research and public service programs were expanded. By the final year of his presidency, the University encompassed some 17,800 students, more than 500 tenured or tenure-track faculty members and 25-plus buildings.

Between Dr. Harold Enarson's resignation the previous summer and Dr. Waetjen's arrival on February 1, 1973, Dr. Harry Newburn (who had briefly led the University from 1965 to 1966) reprised his role as acting president. A number of significant programs and policy measures were adopted during Dr. Newburn's second term, including the Board of Trustees' Affirmative Action Policy Statement and Plan and new fiscal guidelines for student organizations.

In the fall of 1972, CSU launched First College. Offering the benefits of a liberal arts college – including smaller classes and personally designed majors – at an urban university, First College would be a fixture on campus for three decades.

The Women's Comprehensive Program was established in 1977 to increase enrollment and address concerns of female students through recruitment, course development and exit counseling. Dr. Mareyjoyce Green, center, was the program's coordinator from 1977 to 2009.

That same year, the Intramural Sports Center opened on Chester Avenue. Housed beneath a distinctive aluminum exoskeleton (which had to be reinforced after a 1971 blizzard caused a partial roof collapse), the facility included two basketball courts, a training room and laundry facilities, among other amenities.

Dr. Waetjen was elected president by the Board of Trustees on November 9, 1972. Joseph E. Cole, chair of the search committee, told a newspaper reporter that CSU's new leader was "made to order" for the job.

Dr. Waetjen, a Philadelphia native, found success in athletics as well as in academia. He held a bachelor's degree in industrial arts from Millersville

CSU invited political activist Angela Davis to speak November 8, 1972, at the Allen Theatre as part of the University's Assembly and Lecture Series.

The Intramural Sports Center, with its distinctive aluminum exoskeleton, opened in 1972.

Top: The Physical Education Building, dedicated on October 20, 1973, included a gymnasium and a natatorium with an Olympic-sized swimming pool.

Bottom: Musicians perform on the plaza between Rhodes Tower and University Center during University-Community Day in 1979.

University, where he earned varsity letters in boxing (he was the 1939 Golden Gloves light heavyweight boxing champ), football and track, while maintaining a 3.6 GPA.

From 1942 to 1946, he played professional football for the Detroit Lions and the Philadelphia Eagles. Years later, when Dr. Waetjen was named president of CSU, he was asked by a local journalist if an intercollegiate football program at the University might be in the cards. "It's too early to tell," Dr. Waetjen said, adding that intramural sports "give more people a chance to get involved."

When his NFL career was over, he became a public schoolteacher in Philadelphia. He earned a master's degree in vocational education from the University of Pennsylvania and a doctorate in education from the University of Maryland, where he served as vice president of general administration before he came to CSU.

Given its new leader's impressive sports credentials, it was only fitting that the first new building to open under his watch was the Physical Education Building. Dedicated on October 20, 1973, it featured a gymnasium and a natatorium with an Olympic-sized swimming pool (one of only two university indoor pools in Ohio that were 50 meters in length) filled with more than 933,000 gallons of water. The latter venue would go on to host four sold-out NCAA Division I swimming and diving championships and serve as a practice site for U.S. Olympic teams.

University Center, which opened in 1974, was designed to serve as "the gateway to the University."

Up next, just in time for its 10th anniversary, CSU got a new heart.

University Center had its grand opening on October 18, 1974. Looming over Euclid Avenue in the shadow of University Tower, the latest campus addition was billed as "the gateway to the University." It featured a pair of six-story wings that cradled a glass-walled inner courtyard – which soon came to be called "The Cage," for obvious reasons. The new focal point for student activities also featured dining facilities, auditoriums, conference rooms and lounges.

CSU "serves as a key element in the current rebirth of the entire downtown area," said Harry Volk, aide to Cleveland Mayor Ralph Perk, speaking at the University Center dedication ceremony. "It epitomizes, more than any other institution, the greater city that Cleveland is becoming."

The glass-walled inner courtyard of University Center was known as "The Cage."

All the same, greatness proved hard to come by in the next few years. By late 1978, Cleveland – in debt to the tune of $15.5 million in short-term notes – had become the first major American city since the Great Depression to default. A shrinkage of the city's tax base as a result of lost population and lost jobs hastened the financial disaster.

Cleveland's public school system was in disarray, too. In 1976, U.S. District Judge Frank Battisti ruled that the city's schools must be desegregated, which led to crosstown busing.

Little wonder that a popular T-shirt at the time bore the slogan: "Cleveland: You've Got to Be Tough!"

Public service remained a priority for CSU, which established its Maxine Goodman Levin College of Urban Affairs in 1977 and further engaged the community with the Center for Neighborhood Development, as well as a speech and hearing clinic and a legal clinic.

Nonetheless, Dr. Waetjen cautioned against turning to the University as the be-all and end-all solution to all of the city's woes.

"We are not a community problem-solving agency," he said. "We as an institution are not going out to solve the problems of any given industry, government agency or school system directly. We will work to solve problems only as long as we are educating students so they will be skilled in problem-solving."

To this end, students could avail themselves of any number of new academic offerings. Among them were a nursing degree program (whose candidates wore green gowns under white smocks), a bachelor's degree program in physical therapy and an executive MBA program designed to provide advanced managerial skills for seasoned executives.

Research also flourished at the University. Professor John Wilson of the Department of Psychology studied the lingering effects of war experiences on veterans, supported by a Disabled American Veterans grant. Based in part on his influential work, the American Psychiatric Association added post-traumatic stress disorder to the third edition of its *Diagnostic and Statistical Manual of Mental Disorders.* For his work with Vietnam veterans, Dr. Wilson received a presidential commendation from President Jimmy Carter. Other CSU researchers distinguished themselves in other fields. Funded by National Science Foundation grants, Professor

The Maxine Goodman Levin College of Urban Affairs was established in 1977. From left are CSU Vice President for University Relations Clodus Smith, Maxine Goodman Levin and David Meeker, the first person to hold the Albert Levin Chair in Urban Studies and Public Service.

The 1976 recipients of the Distinguished Faculty Awards were (front, from left) Dr. Harry Andrist, Dr. Barry Feinstein, Dr. Roberta Steinbacher and Dr. Joseph Rogus. Standing behind the winners are, from left, J. Maurice Struchen of Society National Bank, CSU Vice President of Academic Affairs John Flower, Dr. Walter Waetjen and Thomas Hannon of Hannon Electric Company (Society National Bank and Hannon Electric Company sponsored the awards).

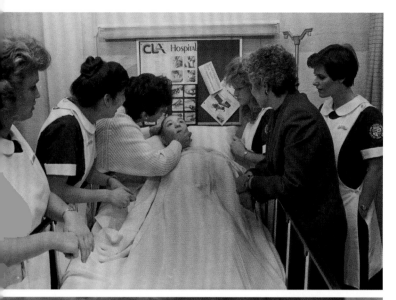

Top: CSU's first nursing students wore forest green uniforms under white smocks.

Bottom: The University's executive MBA program, designed to allow experienced executives to acquire managerial skills without disrupting their careers, held its first classes on September 15, 1980.

C.W. (Paul) Chu of the Department of Physics examined superconductivity in collaboration with a Russian colleague, A.P. (Sasha) Rusakov of Moscow. With the Cold War still in effect, it was "an extremely unusual arrangement between the U.S. and the U.S.S.R.," Dr. Chu noted. Professor Roberta Steinbacher, a founder of the Levin College of Urban Affairs, garnered international attention for her work on the implications of fetal sex preselection. And Professors George Coulman and Gregory Wotzak of the Department of Chemical Engineering conducted research on acid fuel cell technology, with a grant from NASA.

As of 1981, some of the research being done at the University had a new home when the Science and Research Building opened, adding 140,000 square feet of instructional, research and support space. That same year, another CSU landmark got a new name: University Tower was rechristened Rhodes Tower in honor of Governor James Rhodes, who had paved the way for CSU.

When the Cleveland-Marshall College of Law moved into its new campus digs in October 1974, on the northeast corner of Euclid Avenue and East 18th Street, it was nothing short of a royal occasion. Prince Charles presided over the dedication ceremony, received an honorary law degree and flashed a jolly good sense of humor.

"I am amazed by your generosity and perhaps rashness in deciding to confer an honorary degree upon such an eminently unqualified and unlawful candidate," the British dignitary told the crowd at CSU.

The Science and Research Building opened in 1981 with 140,000 square feet of instructional, research and support space.

He wasn't the only high-profile guest to visit the University. Coretta Scott King, widow of the Reverend Dr. Martin Luther King Jr., actually dropped by twice – in April 1980 for a speaking engagement as part of Black Aspirations Week ("Young people are going to have to pick up the mantle of nonviolence," she said) and in June 1985 to receive an honorary doctorate during commencement.

One of the most popular courses during the 1970s was "The Flying Circus of Physics." It was taught by Dr. Jearl Walker, a natural showman who demonstrated scientific principles by walking on hot coals, lying on a bed of nails and sticking his hand into molten lead.

New living arrangements had a significant impact on student life in 1986, when CSU purchased the old Holiday Inn hotel on the southwest corner of Euclid Avenue and East 22nd Street and converted it into a new dormitory: Viking Hall. With 454 beds, it tripled the amount of dorm space at the University, which had been limited to accommodations for 210 resident students in Fenn Tower.

The entire student population, commuters and residents alike, as well as other members of the campus community, found a welcome refuge in the Shire. Taking its name from the fantasy realm conjured by J.R.R. Tolkien of *The Hobbit* and *Lord of the Rings* fame (CSU hosted a conference for Tolkien buffs in 1971), the Shire originally was launched as a coffeehouse in the old Student Center, in the McKee Building. When University Center opened, the Shire relocated to the basement, expanded its menu and packed 'em in for entertainment ranging from musical performances to poetry readings.

Reporter Mary Hirschfeld of *The Plain Dealer* ventured inside circa 1976 to file this dispatch:

It's an Andy Warhol-ish scene with canned music to match, loud enough to drown intimate conversation.

A former Holiday Inn on the southwest corner of Euclid Avenue and East 24th Street, opposite Trinity Cathedral, was reborn in 1986 as Viking Hall.

Pizza is sold by the slice as well as by the pie, and on a recent afternoon none of the T-shirted customers at the counter minded that one of the waitresses had such long, free-hanging locks that when she bent over to pick up the money, they swept lightly across the top of the food and the containers holding the beverages.

Just off campus, clubs in the self-proclaimed "Rock 'n' Roll Capital of the World" also catered to CSU students. At the legendary Agora on East 24th Street, Cleveland's premier music venue, they might catch a "Coffee Break Concert" between classes in the middle of the day or postpone their homework to catch a nighttime gig by the likes of Bruce Springsteen, Bob Marley or the Clash. The Viking Saloon on Chester Avenue, the cradle of a hip underground scene, featured performances by Rocket from the Tombs, Electric Eels and Pere Ubu. And where would CSU be without the Rascal House? The mind shudders to think – and the stomach growls for good measure. Owner Michael Frangos opened this quintessential hangout in a former Burger King restaurant on the southeast corner of Euclid Avenue and East 21st Street in 1980. (It would move just a few blocks west in 2013 to make way for the Center for Innovation in Health Professions.) The Rascal House changed with the changing times, adding – or subtracting, as the case may be – everything from video arcade games to a dance floor to free Wi-Fi, but one thing remained constant: Its pizza could always be counted on to sate the University's masses.

Top: The Shire, seen here circa 1985, in the basement of University Center was a major hub of campus entertainment.

Bottom: A tuition increase of $17 per quarter and an additional $3 per quarter in general fees sparked student protests in 1978.

Krenzler Field opened in 1985. It was named in honor of Alvin Krenzler, a federal judge and former CSU trustee.

Krenzler Field, the first outdoor athletic venue at CSU, opened in August 1985, but the athletics highlight reel was dominated by the 1985-1986 men's basketball team.

Coach Kevin Mackey and his scrappy "run 'n' stun" squad, led by standout point guard Ken "Mouse" McFadden, turned CSU's first trip to the NCAA Tournament in March 1986 into a Cinderella story for the ages. The Vikings were a lowly No. 14 seed, but that didn't stop them from announcing their arrival at "The Big Dance" with a stunning upset over Bobby Knight's third-seeded Indiana Hoosiers in "one of the most indelible games in tournament history," according to *The New York Times*. Sixth-seeded St. Joseph's University fell next to CSU. Advancing to the Sweet 16, the Vikings bowed out with a 71-70 loss to Navy, but not before they had won the hearts of everyone prone to cheering for the underdog.

Paul Stewart, left, and Clinton Ransey celebrate the CSU men's basketball team's victory over St. Joseph's University in the 1986 NCAA Tournament.

Unfortunately, the afterglow proved to be short-lived. Paul Stewart, one of the team's stars, suffered a fatal heart attack during a pickup game a few weeks after the tournament. The NCAA put CSU on probation in 1988 for recruiting violations. Not long afterwards, Mackey fell from grace, the result of well-publicized personal problems.

For a few shining moments there in the thick of that unforgettable March Madness, however, it felt as if everyone in Cleveland and vast legions of fans elsewhere were rooting for the Vikings.

Klaas de Boer coached the CSU men's soccer team from 1972 to 1977, when his squad advanced to the NCAA quarterfinals and de Boer was named coach of the year by the National Soccer Coaches Association of America.

35

By and large, these were good years as CSU came into its own, with no shortage of positive accomplishments in which the University could take pride. Yet tragedy and turmoil also left their marks.

One of the darkest episodes in CSU history transpired over several months in 1982, when three people were murdered on campus. The Reverend Horace Dickerson, Brian Warford and Timothy Sheehan were fatally shot by a neo-Nazi serial killer, who also wounded two other people. After more than 27 years on death row, the convicted murderer was executed in 2011.

The University was rocked again in March 1987, when Cleveland City Council President George Forbes accused CSU of being a racist institution. One month later, with the matter already under federal investigation, a special committee to study racial issues at the University was formed by the Greater Cleveland Roundtable, a nonprofit organization dedicated to improving race relations and minority economic inclusion. The CSU Civic Committee on Race Relations included University students, faculty and administrators, as well as community leaders.

Amid the crisis, Dr. Waetjen announced his resignation.

In October 1987, the University agreed to settle U.S. Department of Labor charges that CSU discriminated against black job applicants and may have underpaid women and black faculty and staff.

As the eventful year drew to a close, the CSU Civic Committee on Race Relations released its findings. According to the report, the University did not adhere to its affirmative action plan, discriminated in hiring and failed to attract and to retain minority students and faculty. The report made several recommendations, including the establishment of a committee on minority affairs at the University, which the CSU Board of Trustees promptly adopted.

"This report has set a constructive tone," said Henry Goodman, chair of the board.

"The recommendations will be addressed in the realistic light of the authority we possess as trustees of CSU, the dollars available to us and the University's multiple responsibilities to this community."

CSU had a framework for going forward, although it would fall to Dr. Waetjen's successor to oversee the healing process.

President

JOHN FLOWER

1988-92

"All Citizens . . . Must Share This Bright Future"

When Dr. John Flower was a young boy, his parents discovered that he had perfect pitch when he correctly identified the precise musical frequency of the whistle on a passing tugboat. He began taking piano lessons when he was five years old, and eventually went on to perform around the globe.

Who better, then, to attempt to bring harmony to Cleveland State University?

Taking the reins on the heels of CSU's longest-serving president, Dr. Walter Waetjen, Dr. Flower had the shortest term in the University's top office: four years. Despite its relative brevity, his presidency was hardly uneventful. It saw CSU undergo a major organizational change in pursuit of positive racial and community relations. His tenure also coincided with the beginning of a transitional period for labor relations at the University, as the classified staff was unionized (followed in later years by the faculty and the professional staff).

Dr. Flower was born and raised in Washington state. During World War II, he was a combat pilot with the U.S. Army Air Corps, stationed in the South Pacific. When his bomber malfunctioned and he became separated from the rest of his squadron, he flew hundreds of miles solo over the ocean from the Philippines to Japan, with only a primitive radio navigation system to guide him.

After the war, he received a bachelor's degree in music composition from the University of Washington. From there, it was off to the University of Michigan, where he earned master's degrees in music theory and piano, as well as a Ph.D. in musicology.

Dr. Flower's academic career led him next to Kent State University, where he was dean of the College of Fine and Professional Arts and associate provost. He joined CSU in 1973 as a professor of music and vice president for academic affairs. He later became provost – and an ivory-tickling provost at that who occasionally gave piano recitals.

Following the departure of Dr. Waetjen, Dr. Flower was appointed interim president in May 1988 and president six months later, although his inauguration ceremony wasn't held until the following spring.

One of his first orders of business was to address the findings of the CSU Civic Committee on Race Relations. In a December 7, 1988, meeting with the Board of Trustees, he outlined plans to hire a minority affairs officer within the next few months and to step up efforts for recruiting and retaining minority employees and students, including a mentoring program for minority first-year students.

Dr. John Flower, an accomplished musician, and CSU music faculty member Joan Terr Ronis teamed up for a series of piano concerts in the early 1980s.

In his "Report of the President to the Board of Trustees on Minority Affairs and Human Relations," Dr. Flower stated:

Cleveland State University is one of the most valuable assets held by the citizens of Greater Cleveland. The total community – black, white, brown, male, female, young or old – shares this asset. Cleveland State holds many of the keys to a bright future for this area. All citizens, regardless of race, gender, religion, must share this brighter future; it must be shared by residents of the city and the suburbs. As Cleveland regenerates itself, it is crucial that all sectors of this community take part in the benefits of our regeneration. Groups of disenfranchised citizens, essentially Black and Hispanic, who do not share in this regeneration stand out starkly as a continuing failure in our system. This cannot continue.

The "regeneration" to which Dr. Flower referred was evident downtown, where the Standard Oil Company (later acquired by BP America), Ohio Bell, and Eaton Corporation had staked their claims in the skyline with new office buildings, the opening of the Galleria at Erieview (soon to be followed by Tower City Center) signaled a resurgence of retail, and the Cleveland Convention Center underwent a major renovation. In some ways, though, there was a tale of two cities to be told. Reporter Keith Sinzinger captured the New Cleveland/Old Cleveland dichotomy of the 1980s in a piece for *The Washington Post*. "The New Cleveland is corporate headquarters, service and professional jobs, downtown construction, recreational and cultural amenities," he wrote. "The Old Cleveland is neighborhoods struggling against decay, double-digit unemployment, racial tension, factory closings, poverty and long-suffering schools."

At CSU, too, there was cause for celebration as well as concern. Enrollment reached an all-time high, with well over 19,000 students, although the University faced formidable financial challenges. With dramatic reductions in government support for Ohio universities, students increasingly bore the brunt of the increased cost of higher education, in the form of skyrocketing tuition. In 1981, for example, state funding accounted for 57 percent of CSU's revenue, while tuition accounted for 37 percent. By 1995, state support had been reduced to just 49 percent of the cost of education, and tuition as a percentage of revenue had increased to 47 percent – a trend that would continue into the 21st century.

While tuition and fee increases were commonplace during this era, so, too, were CSU's efforts to increase tuition assistance funds and the University's endowment, which grew from $2 million to $6 million during Dr. Flower's tenure.

Dr. E. Earl Graham, chair of the Department of Chemical Engineering, gave CSU something else to cheer about when he received the University's first U.S. patent for his trailblazing work in tribology, the study of how sliding surfaces interact. He invented a means of applying a protective coating of organic polymer lubricating film onto a ceramic article, resulting in improved mechanical wear resistance at high temperatures. Dr. Graham's patent was filed in March 1990 and issued two years later.

Student Joel Santana, left, gets a few pointers from Dr. E. Earl Graham, chair of the Department of Chemical Engineering. Dr. Graham was the recipient of CSU's first U.S. patent in 1992.

CSU's reputation as a public research institution was further elevated by a variety of other projects. Dr. Farrokh Alemi and Dr. Richard Stephens were awarded $2.7 million by the National Institute on Drug Abuse to support their efforts to help pregnant women kick cocaine habits and deliver healthy newborns. Dr. Edward (Ned) Hill of the Maxine Goodman Levin College of Urban Affairs made headlines on the front pages of *The New York Times* and *The Wall Street Journal* for his research on inter-state transfer of wealth triggered by the savings and loan crisis. And Professor Patricia Falk of the Cleveland-Marshall College of Law published "Lesbian Mothers: Psychosocial Assumptions in Family Law," a widely cited article examining the disconnect between social science evidence and assumptions made by courts in child custody cases involving lesbian mothers.

By far the biggest milestone to date was CSU's 25th anniversary celebration. It culminated with the "Splash of Silver" gala on September 22, 1990, held inside the new Music and Communication Building and outside under a huge tent.

Formally dedicated one month later, the Music and Communication Building on the northwest corner of Euclid Avenue and East 21st Street was designed by architect Peter van Dijk, whose other credits included Blossom Music Center as well as CSU's Physical Education Building. In addition to a pair of magnificent performance halls, the Music and Communication Building included rehearsal spaces, offices and classrooms. A sculpture titled "Tension Arches" by artist Athena Tacha stood dramatically just outside the entrance.

The groundbreaking ceremony for the Music and Communication Building was held on July 20, 1988. From left are CSU Trustees Gerald Gordon and Henry Goodman; Dr. John Flower; Dr. Leo Jeffries, chair of the communication department; and Dr. James Jones, chair of the music department.

The Music and Communication Building and the "Tension Arches" sculpture by Athena Tacha were dedicated on October 28, 1990.

At the "Splash of Silver" benefit, partygoers dined on swordfish, veal tenderloin and white chocolate desserts shaped like miniature pianos in honor of cabaret singer-pianist Bobby Short, who provided the evening's musical entertainment. He even did an impromptu duet with Dr. Flower.

The gala, which raised $100,000 for CSU's "Foundation for the Future" unrestricted operating fund, drew nearly 700 invited guests – and 100 or so uninvited protesters who staged a show of support for the ousted CSU administrator at the center of what came to be known as "The Winbush Affair."

Dr. Raymond Winbush, the University's first vice president for minority affairs, and CSU parted ways in June 1990 in the wake of a salary dispute. Dr. Winbush, who had been hired the previous year, was the only University vice president who had not been offered a merit raise. After he sought to negotiate higher pay, his contract renewal offer was withdrawn. Dr. Winbush eventually received a severance package from the Board of Trustees, although not before the incident sparked student sit-ins and other demonstrations that lasted several months and reopened old wounds. The Faculty Senate weighed in with a resolution decrying ongoing problems with racism on campus.

The CSU men's basketball team played its first home game in the Convocation Center on December 7, 1991, an exciting occasion despite an 80-61 loss to the University of Michigan.

Speaking at the City Club of Cleveland in April 1991, Dr. Flower said bringing minorities into the mainstream of higher education was the most pressing public policy issue not only at CSU, but at institutions of higher education across the nation. "The urban state university has to retain fidelity to the truth and at the same time learn how to be interactive in the community – without compromising the truth," he said. "That is why I think CSU is a new breed of university. We can't afford to be an ivory tower."

While there clearly was still work to be done with regard to diversity and inclusion, at least one of the University's longstanding dreams came true.

After years and years on the drawing board, the CSU Convocation Center opened in late 1991. Its 13,000-seat arena – the new home court for the University's basketball teams – was adjacent to a 10,000-square-foot conference pavilion.

Dr. John Flower spoke during the Convocation Center dedication ceremony on November 1, 1991.

The first public event at the Convocation Center was a country music double bill on November 3, 1991, featuring Randy Travis and Alan Jackson. Unfortunately, the men's basketball team hit a sour note a few weeks later with its first home game in the new venue, losing 80-61 to the University of Michigan. The future would bring not only rock, pop and hip-hop concerts to the arena (renamed the Wolstein Center in 2005 after Iris Wolstein donated $6.25 million to CSU in memory of her late husband Bert Wolstein, a Cleveland-Marshall graduate), but comedy shows, monster trucks, professional wrestling and even a historic presidential debate.

Another campus addition, Viking Field, opened in 1988. The home of CSU's softball team hosted Horizon League Championships in 1995 and 2003, as well as the 1997 NCAA Play-In Series in which the Vikings defeated Florida A&M to advance to the NCAA Tournament for the first time in CSU softball history.

Top: Alan Jackson (second from right) and Randy Travis (third from right) hold the commemorative first ticket to an event at the Convocation Center: a concert co-headlined by the country singers on November 3, 1991.

Middle: Hispanic Awareness Week has been an annual CSU event since 1990. As part of the festivities in 1991, members of Grupo Cultural Azteca performed in University Center.

Bottom: The 1990-1991 women's fencing team included, from left, Coach Joe Fazekas, Jenny Webber, Michelle Eiben, Erika Karodi and Marianne Jorz. Carlo Songini of the men's fencing team won the NCAA Championship in 1979.

In 1989, CSU purchased the Cleveland Engineering Society Building on Chester Avenue, marking the first campus move east of the Innerbelt. One year later, the building became the Joseph Cole Center for Continuing Education.

In the spring of 1992, the Board of Trustees approved a leave of absence for Dr. Flower, who officially retired in June. Provost J. Taylor Sims was named acting president.

That same year, Dr. Njeri Nuru Holm was hired as vice president for minority affairs and community relations. She succeeded in institutionalizing a number of programs to enhance diversity and inclusion. For example, an important retention and graduation program known as the AHANA initiative targeted African-American, Hispanic, Asian and Native American students but was open to students of all backgrounds. Other retention efforts included STARS (Student Achievement in Research and Scholarship), a program that identified talented undergraduate students and helped to prepare them for academic success at the graduate level.

This kind of programming would continue under CSU's next president, who turned out to be a groundbreaker . . . in *her* own right.

Above: Dr. Louis Milic, standing, and Dr. Leonard Trawick edited *The Gamut,* a magazine published by the Department of English from 1980 to 1992.

Right: Dr. Roberta Steinbacher was a driving force behind the development of the undergraduate degree program in urban studies.

President

CLAIRE VAN UMMERSEN

1993-2001

"Keep the Momentum of Change Going"

Dr. Claire Van Ummersen knew a thing or two about how to rebuild a university.

Shortly before she was named Cleveland State University's fourth president – the first and only woman to hold that position to date – Dr. Van Ummersen spent a week overseas at Kuwait University. There, she led a forum on reviving the school, which sustained heavy damage during the Persian Gulf War.

She would have her work cut out for her at CSU, where she tackled some of the issues that remained unfinished at the end of the previous administration. In the face of a declining pool of college-age students, Dr. Van Ummersen guided the University as it undertook initiatives to improve student services and retention, including the conversion to a semester system. Decreasing levels of financial support from the state led to rapid tuition increases and limited program developments, although Dr. Van Ummersen was able to forge partnerships with other key players in Cleveland.

CSU "as an institution needs to work at developing a more open and diverse approach," she told a reporter when her presidency was announced. "I would hope I would be able to work closely not only with the minority students and faculty, but also the minority community in the city."

A scientist by training, Dr. Van Ummersen got her start in developmental biology, researching the health effects of microwave radiation and how radar affects the eye. A Massachusetts native, she earned her bachelor's, master's and doctoral degrees in biology at Tufts University. She went on to hold a variety of faculty and leadership positions at the University of Massachusetts before assuming leadership roles with the Board of Regents of Higher Education for Massachusetts and the University System of New Hampshire.

Dr. Van Ummersen took office at CSU on April 20, 1993. Three months later, in her first speech as president of CSU, she spoke at the City Club of Cleveland about challenges facing institutions of higher education at the end of the 20th century, including diminished state and federal aid. "Public higher-education institutions are caught between the proverbial rock and hard place," she said. "Most students today need help financially and academically in order to enroll and successfully complete a higher-education degree."

Dr. Claire Van Ummersen, left, and Cleveland Mayor Jane Campbell, a CSU alumna, attended a groundbreaking ceremony for the 17th–18th Street Block Project, which included new buildings for the College of Business and the College of Urban Affairs, as well as expanded library facilities for the College of Law.

At CSU, tuition and fee increases continued apace with the decreases in state and federal funding and increases in the cost of living. New scholarships were established, including the Ahuja Endowed Scholarship Fund in Business Administration and Engineering, the Herman David Memorial Scholarship in Law, the Joan Terr Ronis Memorial Scholarship (endowed by Mu Phi Epsilon) and the Claire Van Ummersen Presidential Scholarship.

Like her presidential predecessors as well as those who would come after her, Dr. Van Ummersen also wielded a shovel from time to time. She was joined by Ohio Governor George Voinovich and other dignitaries at the October 1994 groundbreaking for the so-called 17th-18th Street Block Project. The ambitious venture, scheduled to be completed in three phases, entailed new buildings for the James Nance College of Business Administration (Monte

The new College of Business was dedicated on June 2, 1998. The following year, it was named Monte Ahuja Hall in honor of CSU trustee and alumnus Monte Ahuja.

Guests gathered in the lobby of PlayhouseSquare's Palace Theatre on March 3, 1999, for the groundbreaking ceremony for the College of Urban Affairs building.

The Health Sciences Building was dedicated during a ribbon-cutting ceremony on October 27, 1999. From left are Dr. William Shorrock, CSU Trustee Monte Ahuja, Ohio State Senator Grace Drake, Dr. Claire Van Ummersen, Dr. Andrew Miracle and College of Arts and Sciences Dean Karen Steckol.

Ahuja Hall opened in 1998) and the Maxine Good-man Levin College of Urban Affairs (Glickman-Miller Hall opened in 2001), as well as an expanded library (which opened in 1998) for the Cleveland-Marshall College of Law and a new parking garage.

"The project emphasizes the urban nature of the University," Dr. Van Ummersen said. "Further, it develops another entire block of the city, making a contribution to the renaissance of downtown Cleveland."

Five years later, she presided over a ribbon-cutting ceremony for the new Health Sciences Building, a two-story, underground structure south of the Physical Education Building and west of Mather Mansion. In another health-related matter, the Board of Trustees voted during Dr. Van Ummersen's tenure to prohibit smoking in all University buildings, with the exception of dorm rooms in Viking Hall. (By 2013, the entire campus would be smoke-free.)

In the fall of 1998, CSU adopted a new academic calendar, switching from quarters to semesters after several years of planning and input from students, faculty and staff. It was hoped that the conversion would make it easier for students to transfer coursework among schools, the majority of which were on semester schedules. Faculty leaders praised Dr. Van Ummersen for her handling of the switch, although CSU put off a corresponding adjustment from a dominant four-credit-hour curriculum to a dominant three-credit-hour curriculum until 2014.

Another major transition proved anything but smooth. As organizations around the world upgraded computer systems to avoid Y2K crashes and ensure a smooth transition into the new millennium, CSU purchased PeopleSoft software in 1997 to manage financial aid, among other functions. Glitches with the system soon led to a chorus of complaints from students, faculty and staff as well as frustrating delays, with thousands of students left waiting for months to receive financial aid. The upgrade was "a recipe for disaster," in the words of a 1999 report issued by the Ohio Inspector General. The University eventually sued PeopleSoft (later acquired by the Oracle Corporation) for breach of contract and fraud. A settlement was reached in 2005, with Oracle agreeing to pay $4.25 million to CSU, which covered the University's losses and helped to fund the creation of the Honors Student Scholarship Endowment.

These widely publicized software woes overshadowed some of the era's more positive achievements, including new partnerships with other Cleveland institutions. In 1998, CSU and the Cleveland Clinic Foundation established a collaboration for a joint doctoral program in applied biomedical engineering between the Fenn College of Engineering and the Lerner Research Institute. Doctoral students took courses at the University and conducted research at the Cleveland Clinic, while receiving financial support from both institutions.

CSU teamed up with Kent State University, the Northeastern Ohio Universities Colleges of Medicine and Pharmacy and the University of Akron to create a master of public health program. CSU also developed articulation agreements with community colleges, aligning courses so that students could transfer without losing credits. CSU's Advanced

Manufacturing and Learning Center (which provided development assistance and workforce training for manufacturers) expanded its partnerships, too, which created more opportunities for students to gain hands-on experience.

CSU and the University of Akron jointly offered a master's degree in social work – the first Ohio degree available via distance learning. CSU also utilized distance learning to offer Advanced Placement courses for high school students.

The scholarly work and research of CSU faculty yielded more highlights. Nearly 2,000 miles from Northeast Ohio, in a remote section of Belize, Dr. Peter Dunham of the Department of Anthropology discovered four Maya cities in a mountain jungle in 1993, where pre-Columbian civilization flourished more than 1,000 years earlier. Among the ruins were plazas, monuments and an ancient ball court. Dr. Dunham, director of the Maya Mountains Archaeological Project, received major research grants from the National Geographic Society for his work.

Dr. William Morgan of the College of Arts and Sciences was the principal investigator on CSU's first R01 Grant from the National Institutes of Health, which provided more than $2 million to fund his research on drug-addicted mothers and their children. Dr. Michael Kalafatis of the Department of Chemistry received a $300,000 award from the American Heart Association in support of his work on the biochemistry of blood coagulation and thrombosis. And Masumi Hayashi of the Department of Art, a photographer renowned for

her panoramic photo collages, was the recipient of the Cleveland Arts Prize and two Ohio Arts Council Fellowships.

In 2000, University officials toyed with the idea of changing CSU's name to "The University of Cleveland." It wasn't the first time that a new moniker had been considered, although the latest proposal generated some buzz. *The Plain Dealer* reported that an unnamed source close to the Board of Trustees said removing the "State" from "Cleveland State University" would underscore CSU's commitment to Cleveland. As in the past, though, the name change never made it past the discussion stage.

Another rechristening went off without a hitch. In October 1999, CSU's celebrated swimming facility was renamed the Robert Busbey Natatorium. Busbey was a four-sport athlete at Fenn College (baseball, fencing, swimming and track) and the college's

The Robert Busbey Natatorium, named in honor of former CSU Athletic Director Robert Busbey (second from right), was dedicated on October 2, 1999.

first All-American. He served as the college's head swimming coach and also coached track and golf. He also was named assistant swimming coach for the 1964 U.S. Olympic Team. He continued to coach swimming after Fenn College became CSU, where he succeeded Homer Woodling as director of athletics in 1966. Over the course of 24 years, Busbey grew CSU's athletics program into a formidable contender. He became associate vice president for athletic affairs in 1990 and retired four years later.

The 1996 Olympic Games in Atlanta had a noteworthy Viking connection: Matt Ghaffari, who had a stellar collegiate career a decade earlier when he wrestled at CSU. He was one of three Viking wrestlers to qualify for the 1984 NCAA Championships. As of this writing, Ghaffari still held the University record for most pins in a single season: 14. Twelve years after he graduated from CSU, he won the Olympic silver medal in Greco-Roman wrestling (super-heavyweight division). The former Viking standout became the only U.S. wrestler to win a combined four Olympic and World medals.

President Bill Clinton and Vice President Al Gore showed off their new CSU sweatshirts backstage at the Wolstein Center, where they held a campaign rally on the eve of Election Day 1996.

In addition to CSU events, the Convocation Center continued to host a wide range of other activities, including the first rounds of the NCAA Men's Basketball Championship in 2000 and 2005 and a campaign rally co-headlined by President Bill Clinton and Vice President Al Gore on the eve of Election Day 1996. The candidates were given CSU sweatshirts as well as another special gift: a reunion performance by the James Gang, the classic-rock trio led by singer-guitarist Joe Walsh. "It's about time they got back together," President Clinton said. "That's what we're about – bringing people back together."

On another memorable occasion, Cleveland-born comedian Drew Carey dropped by the Convocation Center in May 2000 to receive an honorary doctorate from CSU and to deliver the commencement address. He urged graduates to set goals and work hard to achieve them. Oh, and one more thing: "Don't forget to tip your professors on the way out!"

Toward the end of her tenure – which saw the Board of Trustees approve the undergraduate degree program in women's studies and adopt the Sexual Harassment Policy Statement – Dr. Van Ummersen addressed a CSU committee on the role and status of women in higher education. Also in attendance were the female presidents of four other Northeast Ohio institutions: Carol Cartwright of Kent State University, Anne Deming of Notre Dame College, Sister Diana Stano of Ursuline College and Jerry Sue Thornton of Cuyahoga Community College.

Dr. Van Ummersen urged the gathering to provide mentoring and support for women.

"Every one of us can take a step to open the door for another woman," she said. "I see women not being replaced by other women. We move forward and we step back. . . . We need leaders to keep the momentum of change going."

In November 2000, Dr. Van Ummersen announced that she would step down by the following June. She had accepted a position with the American Council on Education, as vice president and director of the Office of Women in Higher Education.

During her time at CSU, the forward momentum in Cleveland was palpable. Yes, the city still struggled under the weight of serious socioeconomic issues, including high unemployment and low graduation rates for high school students. But other developments – including gleaming new downtown attractions such as the Gateway sports complex (where the Cleveland Indians came *this* close to winning the 1995 World Series) and the Rock and Roll Hall of Fame and Museum – seemed to impart a glow that had been missing in Cleveland for too long.

"Cities have great wealth because of their 'richness,' not simply because they are rich!" wrote Don Iannone, director of the Economic Development Program in the Levin College of Urban Affairs, in a 1995 op-ed piece about Cleveland's rebirth. "That richness is a product of our diversity, our aspirations, our shared experiences and traditions. We have it."

With the revival came a newfound respect. Cleveland was hailed in the media as "the new American city" and "the comeback city." As it turned out, CSU also was ready to turn a corner.

President

MICHAEL SCHWARTZ

2001-09

"We Are Going to Have Some Fun"

Dr. Michael Schwartz liked to joke that regardless of his other achievements, he was destined to be remembered as the man who put "CSU" atop Rhodes Tower.

He did indeed have those letters affixed – in radiant green, lit up at night – on each side of the campus landmark's parapet, for all of Cleveland to see. But the fifth president of Cleveland State University also raised CSU's profile and bolstered its reputation in many other ways. Under his leadership, the University engaged in an ambitious strategic planning process that renewed and reinvigorated CSU's physical space, academic programs and relationships with external partners.

A bold master plan transformed the formerly austere, inward-looking campus into a more vibrant and welcoming home of higher education in the heart of Cleveland. Embracing the slogan "The city is our campus" and the philosophy that for Cleveland to be good, CSU must be good, Dr. Schwartz was the catalyst who made the University an integral player in the economic growth of its hometown. His vision extended to raising academic standards, reengineering student services and restructuring CSU to run as a business, with proper emphasis on the "customers" of the University – its students.

Born and raised in Chicago, Dr. Schwartz earned a bachelor's degree in psychology, a master's degree in industrial relations and a Ph.D. in psychology from the University of Illinois at Urbana-Champaign. He served on the faculties of Wayne State University, Indiana University and Florida Atlantic University before settling at Kent State University, where he held a succession of leadership positions prior to assuming the KSU presidency from 1982 to 1991.

The CSU Board of Trustees tapped Dr. Schwartz to serve as the University's interim president in May 2001. He became president six months later.

"Education that does not lead to action is education that in a terrible way has been wasted," Dr. Schwartz said during his inaugural address. "A mission without passion soon becomes a dull-witted mantra. . . . We are going to take some risks. We are going to have some fun at Cleveland State University."

Fenn Tower opened as a campus residence hall on August 15, 2006.

In revitalizing CSU, Dr. Schwartz also hoped that the University would play an important role in revitalizing Cleveland. The new millennium found the city caught up in what *The Plain Dealer* called the "Quiet Crisis." During the second half of the 20th century, Cleveland had lost nearly half its population and more than half of its manufacturing jobs, which historically was its top job-producing sector. Downtown redevelopment in the 1990s was a step in the right direction, but it certainly wasn't a panacea.

A wake-up call was sounded in 2004, when Cleveland was declared the poorest large city in America. According to a U.S. Census Bureau report, income for nearly one-third of Cleveland residents fell below the federal poverty level: $18,660 for a family of four. Even more sobering was the news that nearly half of the city's children lived in poverty.

"Unaddressed social needs have a way of undoing the best-laid plans of architects and planners," wrote the framers of the "Connecting Cleveland 2020 Citywide Plan," released in 2007. "It is clear that 'place-based' strategies addressing land use and physical development must be coupled with 'people-based' strategies that address people's needs for connections to education, jobs, services, recreation and the arts, as well as the need for 'connectedness' to neighbors and to a supportive community."

In the 21st century, Cleveland faced a host of challenges and opportunities, the authors of the civic-vision document noted. "Among the most pressing is the accelerating shift toward a knowledge-based economy – both a challenge and an opportunity for a city struggling to educate its children, yet rich in institutions of higher learning," they wrote.

"Cleveland, however, is a resilient city that has the ability to use the assets it built during its peak years to reinvent itself as a competitive place to live and do business for generations to come."

Among these assets, the plan listed CSU.

The University was pursuing a "Building Blocks for the Future" master plan of its own, which included $350 million in new construction and renovations. As CSU answered the call to become more connected to the community, its evolving campus embraced and elevated the surrounding cityscape.

On August 15, 2006, the University celebrated the grand opening of a new residence hall: Fenn Tower. The Art Deco holdover from the Fenn College days now boasted apartment-style dorm rooms, complete with kitchenettes and high-speed Internet access. The upgrades doubled CSU's capacity for resident students to 900 beds.

"In order for us to grow, we have to go outside the immediate commuting area," Jack Boyle, a driving force behind the campus makeover in his role as CSU's vice president of business affairs and finance, told a reporter. "That requires more dorm capacity."

Above: The 110,000-square-foot Recreation Center opened on August 28, 2006, providing the campus community with basketball courts, a multipurpose gym, fitness areas, a 1/10-mile indoor track and more. Below: For some, workouts at the Recreation Center stretched into the night.

It also entailed other amenities. Just days after Fenn Tower welcomed its new inhabitants, the new Recreation Center opened on the south side of Chester Avenue. It featured a main gym with two basketball courts, a multipurpose gym, fitness areas for cardiovascular workouts and weight training, racquetball and squash courts and a 1/10-mile indoor track. The Recreation Center quickly found favor not only with the CSU community, but members of the community at large, too, establishing itself as one of downtown Cleveland's premier fitness facilities.

In 2007, Dr. Schwartz and other members of the University's leadership team got a new space of their own with the opening of the Parker Hannifin Administration Center on Euclid Avenue. The restaurant on its ground floor, Elements Bistro, showcased Northeast Ohio fare and soon became a popular lunch destination. Across the Administration Center's courtyard, Parker Hannifin Hall – home of the Office of Research and the College of Graduate Studies – opened the following year.

The architectural reboot also brought a new look to the Main Classroom Building, a campus mainstay since 1970. Back then, much of its first floor was an open plaza that became a wind tunnel in the winter. As part of the Main Classroom Building renovation,

The Parker Hannifin Administration Center, right, and Parker Hannifin Hall, left, opened in 2007 and 2008, respectively. The latter building combined historic Howe Mansion with a three-story addition.

the first floor was enclosed, creating new space for a computer lab, eateries and offices. The building also boasted a curvaceous new glass façade that afforded a sweeping view of campus, with the Cleveland skyline as a backdrop.

Other buildings had outlived their usefulness. University Center was razed in 2008 to make way for a new Student Center. "The Cage" was history.

CSU also opened its first satellite campuses, with suburban facilities in Westlake (in 2003) and in Solon (in 2004; it closed seven years later) offering courses for undergraduates and graduates, as well as continuing-education workshops.

Renovations to the Main Classroom Building in 2007 included a new glass façade and the enclosure of the first floor plaza.

The outward manifestations across campus of a new CSU taking shape were accompanied by equally dynamic changes to academic programming, including new academic standards, an honors program, an undergraduate research program, a common reading program, learning communities and revamped general education requirements. Since its inception, the University had admitted all graduates of Ohio high schools on a first-come, first-served basis. This changed in 2006, when CSU implemented more rigorous admission standards in hopes of improving academic performance and retention. The new criteria included at least a 2.3 high school GPA and a 750 on the SAT or 16 on the ACT.

The honors program enrolled its first class of 40 students in the fall of 2004. The Honors Student Scholarship Endowment was established using the PeopleSoft settlement funds.

Among the other programs launched during Dr. Schwartz's presidency were the Middle Eastern studies program, the Center for School Leadership, the International Business Program and programs to improve the bar passage rate for Cleveland-Marshall College of Law students.

In 2004, the College of Arts and Sciences was reconfigured into two academic divisions: the College of Liberal Arts and Social Sciences and the College of Science. The following year, collaborations between CSU and the Cleveland Clinic expanded to include not only the joint doctoral program in applied biomedical engineering, but also programs in clinical/bioanalytical chemistry and regulatory biology.

Top: Dr. Michael Schwartz addressed attendees in the Main Classroom Building atrium during the Student Center ground-breaking ceremony on October 16, 2008.

Bottom: CSU launched its women's soccer program in 2004.

The 2004 approval of the Master of Fine Arts in Creative Writing (NEOMFA) – a joint degree program supported by Kent State University, the University of Akron, Youngstown State University and CSU – and the 2006 opening of CSU's Center for eLearning indicated a willingness on the University's part to consider alternatives to traditional models of course content delivery, at both the undergraduate and graduate levels.

The Confucius Institute at CSU was established through a partnership among the University, the Office of Chinese Language Council International (Hanban) and Beijing's Capital University of Economics and Business. The Confucius Institute is dedicated to enhancing the local community's understanding of Chinese language, culture and business.

CSU also sought to improve student services. Campus411 opened in 2004 as a one-stop center prepared to assist students with questions regarding admissions, academic records, financial aid, registration and student accounts. It also provided referrals to other student-support offices. Originally located in University Center, Campus411 later set up shop in the Main Classroom Building.

Enrollment Services launched Campus411 in 2004 as a one-stop center for student services.

The University made fundraising a priority, especially in relation to student scholarships. This was, in part, a response to ongoing cuts to state funding for higher education.

"We have gone from state-supported to state-assisted to merely state-located," Dr. Schwartz said during his 2002 inaugural address.

Significantly, after approving increases in instructional fees in excess of 10 percent in 2003 and additional increases for a variety of fees in subsequent years, the Board of Trustees approved holding tuition at current rates in 2008, during the "Great Recession," and then voted to approve an overall tuition freeze for undergraduate, graduate and law students.

By 2009, the final year of Dr. Schwartz's presidency, the state share of instruction amounted to only 37 percent of CSU's budget revenue sources, while student instructional fees accounted for 56 percent. During that same year, total gifts for scholarships equaled $8.3 million, an increase of 16 percent over the previous five years, and endowments totaled $32 million, a 42 percent increase over a five-year period.

Major gifts of this era included a commitment of $5 million from Iris Wolstein in memory of her husband, Bert Wolstein, to support a renovation for the Cleveland-Marshall College of Law and a $1.25

million challenge-pledge to
support the creation of the
Bert and Iris Wolstein Endowed
Scholarship Fund. Parker
Hannifin Corporation made a
$4 million gift commitment to
support student scholarships
and building improvements.
The Joseph and Martha Peck
Estate contributed $1.5 million
for student scholarships.

Top: Trustees renamed the Convocation
Center in honor of CSU benefactors Bert
and Iris Wolstein in 2005.

Right: Guests mingle during the Wolstein
Center dedication festivities on November
18, 2005.

As Dr. Schwartz, whose presidency began just after the 9/11 terrorist attacks, prepared to step down, the G.I. Bill of 2009 went into effect. A key support program for veterans also came into being at CSU when the Walmart Foundation made a $100,000 contribution to launch Supportive Education for the Returning Veteran (SERV). As the University's 50th anniversary approached, there were approximately 600 student veterans on campus, representing all five branches of the armed forces. Almost half were post-9/11 veterans, and about 30 percent were women. SERV eventually was replaced by the Veteran Student Success Program, dedicated to helping veterans make the most of their college experience and graduate in the shortest time possible.

CSU's Center for Gene Regulation in Health and Disease (GRHD) was launched in 2008 with funding from the Ohio Third Frontier Commission's Ohio Research Scholars Program. GRHD's faculty members – representing the physics; chemistry; and biological, geological and environmental sciences departments – were involved in extensive collaborative networks that included the Cleveland Clinic and Case Western Reserve University, as well as other leading national and international institutions. GRHD has become one of the top gene-research centers in the United States, earning nearly $15 million in funding to date and publishing more than 100 papers.

The center exemplified Dr. Schwartz's faith in the abilities of the CSU faculty. "The professors are the most powerful tools of economic development this region has," he said.

Dr. Zhiqiang Gao, associate professor of electrical and computer engineering, developed patented motion-control technology that was sublicensed to Texas Instruments by Linestream Technologies Inc., the first CSU spinout company to receive more than $5 million in venture capital funding. His energy-saving innovation stood to benefit manufacturers of motor-controlled products ranging from washing machines to medical equipment.

CSU faculty members distinguished themselves outside the laboratory, too. Dr. Angelin Chang, a professor of piano and coordinator of keyboard studies in the Department of Music, won a Grammy Award in 2007 for her recording of "Oiseaux Exotiques" with the Cleveland Chamber Symphony. Her CSU colleague David Yost was the project's recording engineer.

CSU music professor Angelin Chang won a Grammy Award in 2007 for her recording of "Oiseaux Exotiques" with the Cleveland Chamber Symphony. *Photo by Janet Macoska.*

CSU hosted a historic debate at the Wolstein Center on February 26, 2008, between Democratic presidential candidates Hillary Clinton and Barack Obama, seen here with debate co-moderator Tim Russert of NBC News, a Cleveland-Marshall College of Law alumnus.

The eyes of the nation and much of the rest of the world were on CSU on February 26, 2008, when the Wolstein Center hosted a historic debate between Democratic presidential candidates Hillary Clinton and Barack Obama. For good measure, one of the moderators was a Cleveland-Marshall alumnus: Tim Russert of NBC News. Pundits were divided as to which candidate had emerged victorious, although *The Plain Dealer* declared CSU the true winner: "On the night Hillary Clinton and Barack Obama went to college in Cleveland, the best grade in the class belonged to the school that hosted them." Remarkably, the debate wasn't finalized until February 12, giving the University only two weeks to work out all the logistics, including technical issues related to the broadcast, credentials for some 600 journalists and background checks for 1,600 ticketed spectators and 500 volunteers.

One year later, athletics was back in the spotlight as the men's basketball team (coached by Gary Waters, who came to CSU in 2006, and led by future NBA point guard Norris Cole) returned to the NCAA Tournament for the first time since the magical Sweet 16 appearance of 1986. Twenty-three years later, the No. 13 seed Vikings pulled off another first-round upset, defeating No. 4 seed Wake Forest, before bowing out with a loss to the Arizona Wildcats in the second round.

As a standout on the Vikings men's basketball team from 2007 to 2011, Norris Cole set the record for games played (140), among other achievements. A first-round pick in the 2011 NBA draft, he went on to win NBA Championships with the Miami Heat in 2012 and 2013.

In 2005, a removable, air-supported dome was erected over Krenzler Field, providing an indoor practice facility for multiple sports during the winter months.

This era also witnessed the rise and fall (and rise and fall, rise and fall, rise and fall, etc.) of a new CSU athletics star: the Krenzler Field Dome. It made its debut in December 2005 and was removed the following May. The air-supported, 60-foot-high dome turned the field into a year-round facility not only for soccer, but also for baseball, softball and cross-country. Every winter, the dome went up. Every spring, it came down.

Summing up everything that the University stood for in just a couple of words might seem like a tall order, but two words eloquently and succinctly told the tale:

"Engaged Learning."

Introduced in 2008 by Assistant Vice President of University Marketing Rob Spademan, the tagline became synonymous with CSU.

"Engaged Learning is our brand promise, but it's really our purpose as a University," Spademan said. "Every day, students experience Engaged Learning opportunities made possible by CSU's unique location in the heart of the city, its partnerships with world-class health facilities, businesses, educational institutions and arts and civic organizations and its faculty research that is providing solutions to real-world challenges."

The motto put a fresh spin on the hands-on approach to higher education that CSU had embraced all along. Furthermore, it underscored the University's ongoing connectivity with Cleveland.

When Dr. Schwartz retired in June 2009, Engaged Learning was more than a legacy. It was a destiny waiting to be fulfilled anew.

President

RONALD M. BERKMAN

2009–PRESENT

"In and of This City"

When Dr. Ronald M. Berkman became the sixth president of Cleveland State University, Cleveland was a much different place than it had been when CSU was founded 45 years earlier.

In the 1960s, Cleveland was the eighth largest city in the United States. As the first decade of the 21st century drew to a close, Cleveland wasn't even in the Top 40. Its population had plunged to 396,800 – the lowest in a century – according to Census 2010. In addition to population loss, the city had survived a familiar Rust Belt double-whammy: loss of core industrial economy and loss of jobs.

Under the radar, however, a decidedly more positive picture was emerging. Among the researchers who brought it into focus was Richey Piiparinen, director of the Center for Population Dynamics at the Maxine Goodman Levin College of Urban Affairs. In a series of eye-opening reports, he documented the makings of a Rust Belt renaissance – with CSU's hometown poised to play a starring role.

Brain gain in Cleveland is real, Piiparinen and his colleagues declared. They found that between 2000 and 2012, the metropolitan area gained more than 60,000 people, age 25 and over, with a college degree. From 2006 to 2012 alone, the number of college-educated 25- to 34-year-olds in Cleveland increased 23 percent. Across the same age group, Cleveland was No. 8 in the nation for workers with an advanced degree, ahead of the likes of Chicago and Seattle.

The data pointed toward a resurgent metropolis ready to enter the upper echelon of the new knowledge economy.

This tremendous potential was not lost on Dr. Berkman. He came to CSU with a deep background in urban affairs, having written extensively about topics ranging from municipal government to public policy to economic development. Along with a sweeping series of student-success initiatives, a steadfast commitment to tightening CSU's ties to Cleveland would become a hallmark of his administration, which ushered in an era of record-setting first-year classes, curriculum improvements and forward-thinking partnerships with other Northeast Ohio institutions.

"Cleveland State University is in and of this city, and the connections and bonds between the two of them must be strengthened," Dr. Berkman said during his inaugural address on October 16, 2009. "We must build bridges between the University and the city that will provide environments for students to apply and expand what they are learning in the classroom and the laboratory."

In distilling the essence of Engaged Learning, he emphasized engagement with Cleveland itself as an integral component of CSU's core philosophy.

A native of Brooklyn, New York, Dr. Berkman earned a bachelor's degree in political science from William Paterson College and a Ph.D. in political science from Princeton University. Prior to assuming the presidency at CSU, he held various leadership positions at Florida International University, including provost, executive vice president and chief operating officer. He previously had taught at the Woodrow Wilson School at Princeton, Brooklyn College and the City University of New York (CUNY) Graduate Center, and had served as a visiting professor at the University of California at Berkeley, New York University and the University of Puerto Rico.

He was no stranger to CSU, either. Dr. Berkman had visited the University in the early 1990s to attend a conference, where he presented a paper titled "Urban Universities and Urban Government."

When the CSU Board of Trustees needed to fill the big shoes left by Dr. Schwartz, Dr. Berkman was the unanimous choice. He, in turn, was excited about the prospect of building upon the forward momentum created by the previous administration and taking the University to even greater heights. CSU "was on a launch pad," he told *Cleveland Magazine.*

Nonetheless, significant challenges would have to be addressed before the University was cleared for liftoff.

As a first-generation college student himself who had paid his way through college by driving a beer truck and working in a gypsum factory, Dr. Berkman knew firsthand about the struggles faced by students who worked as hard outside the classroom as they worked in the classroom in pursuit of a degree. Streamlining their path toward graduation was a top priority of his administration.

In response to growing concerns about the need to improve retention and graduation rates at public universities in Ohio, the Board of Trustees approved a Graduation Incentive Plan, devised by Dr. Berkman, that offers a 2 percent tuition rebate and $100 per semester in book expenses to undergraduate students who complete their academic year in good standing with at least 30 credit hours.

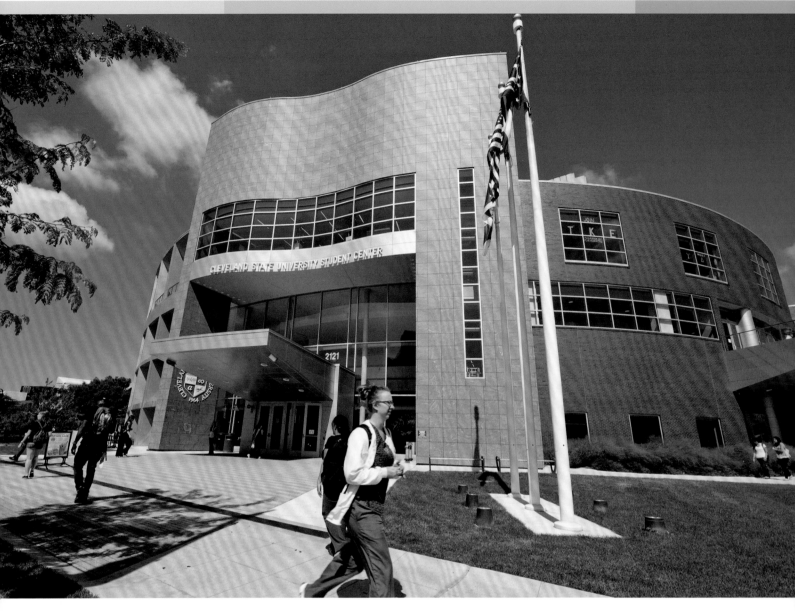

The new Student Center, designed by renowned architect Charles Gwathmey, was dedicated September 8, 2010.

The plan was one of several student-success measures implemented to save money and time for students. Other initiatives included an online degree audit program, multiterm registration for students to plan their entire academic year in advance and a 120-credit-hour standard for graduation that coincided with "The Big Switch," CSU's adoption of a dominant three-credit-hour curriculum starting in 2014.

Amid the heightened emphasis on student success, student life flourished as two major projects came to fruition.

At the very heart of campus, facing Euclid Avenue with a stunning façade of glass and granite, the new Student Center was dedicated September 8, 2010. Designed to foster interaction and to promote community, the three-story hub of student activity at CSU was one of the last masterpieces created by the late Charles Gwathmey, a renowned New York City architect whose other projects included an addition to the Guggenheim Museum.

Only a few days earlier, the Euclid Commons residence hall complex opened on East 24th Street, which was extended to connect Euclid Avenue and Prospect Avenue. On the same corner where the old CSU bookstore had stood for decades, stacks of textbooks and racks of apparel were replaced by smartly appointed apartment-style accommodations for some 600 resident students.

The Euclid Commons residence hall opened in 2010.

Julka Hall, home of the College of Education and Human Services as well as the School of Nursing, was named in honor of alumnus Anand "Bill" Julka and his wife, Neeraj.

The new home of the College of Education and Human Services as well as the School of Nursing also opened in 2010. Julka Hall was named in honor of Smart Solutions Inc. founder and CSU alumnus Anand "Bill" Julka and his wife, Neeraj.

These dramatic new buildings represented the culmination of a $500 million campus makeover. It was said that CSU graduates who hadn't been back in 10 years or more wouldn't recognize the place. Others marveled at the transformation, too. "If there were a prize in Northeast Ohio for the most-improved college or university campus, Cleveland State University would win it hands down," declared Steven Litt, *The Plain Dealer*'s architecture critic.

The Langston was the largest residential development in Cleveland in 30 years. It opened in two phases, in 2012 and 2013.

As some buildings rose, others were reduced to rubble. Viking Hall was razed in 2012 to make way for the Center for Innovation in Medical Professions. Scheduled to open in 2015, the latest iconic addition to campus was designed to bring CSU's health-related programs together in one collaborative space, housing the CSU Health and Wellness Clinic, a speech and hearing clinic, audiology labs, nursing labs and occupational therapy/physical therapy training rooms, among other amenities. The center also was set to include the headquarters of the NEOMED-CSU Partnership for Urban Health, a joint venture between Northeast Ohio Medical University and CSU to enhance training for an urban-focused health-care workforce.

The revitalization evident throughout CSU also radiated into the surrounding neighborhood. Along Chester Avenue, the Langston complex (aka Campus Village) was the largest residential development in Cleveland in 30 years. It opened in two phases, in 2012 and in 2013, bringing a total of 700-plus new apartments to the Campus District.

Wielding shovels at the groundbreaking ceremony for the Center for Innovation in Medical Professions on December 9, 2013, were, from left, CSU Board of Trustees Chairman Robert Rawson Jr., Dr. Ronald M. Berkman, NEOMED President Jay Gershen and Cleveland Mayor Frank Jackson.

As the number of resident students at CSU hit an all-time high, new traditions were born. With Fenn Tower and Euclid Commons filled to capacity, Move-In Day established itself as an August ritual. Up and down East 24th Street, a steady stream of vehicles deposited wave after wave of campus dwellers by the hundreds, toting dollies loaded with books, clothes and untold quantities of ramen noodles.

Old traditions were reborn, too. In 2012, for the first time since the 1960s, CSU had a Homecoming Parade, with Dr. Berkman and Cleveland Mayor Frank Jackson (a three-time CSU alumnus) leading a colorful procession of students and alumni across campus. The parade returned in 2013 and in 2014, bigger and better than ever.

With all this excitement in the air, was it any wonder Emmy Award-winning actress Betty White enrolled at CSU? Well, not really – but her character on the hit TV Land sitcom "Hot in Cleveland" did start taking classes at the University, unexpectedly raising CSU's profile in front of a national audience.

At least one tradition remained elusive, however: There would be no football at CSU. Toward the end of his tenure, Dr. Schwartz had floated the idea of fielding a Vikings football team. A consultant estimated it would cost between $13 million and $15 million to launch the program, and $1 million annually to operate. The idea was sacked after a 2010 poll found that although a majority of students wanted football at CSU, most would not be willing to pay extra fees to support it.

Undaunted, the bookstore sold a popular line of "CSU Football" T-shirts and hoodies that proudly proclaimed: "UNDEFEATED SINCE 1964."

Then again, other Vikings teams gave fans plenty to cheer about. In 2013, for the second time in five years, CSU won the McCafferty Trophy, awarded annually to the top overall sports program in the Horizon League. The honor came on the heels of an outstanding 2012-2013 campaign for the Vikings, which brought Horizon League championships for the women's volleyball team and the men's swimming and diving, soccer and tennis teams.

Vikings also excelled in the classroom. During this era, more than half of CSU's student-athletes consistently maintained a 3.0 GPA or better.

More milestones were achieved in 2014, including a 10th place finish in the NCAA regional tournament for the men's golf team – its best yet – and a CSU record for Gary Waters, who became the all-time winningest coach in the history of the men's basketball program when he notched his 150th victory with a win by the Vikings over Eastern Illinois University.

Coach Waters still had a way to go, though, before he would catch the all-time winningest coach in the history of CSU Athletics: Wally Morton. He stepped down as head coach of the men's and women's swimming and diving teams in February 2014, with 385 victories to his credit over a career spanning nearly 40 years. His teams won two Horizon League championships, two Midwestern Collegiate Conference titles and 14 Penn-Ohio championships. He also coached five athletes who qualified for the NCAA championships.

Jakub Dobies finished 13th in the 100-meter breaststroke at the 2009 NCAA Championships, becoming the first CSU and Horizon League swimmer to earn All-American honors.

CSU also had much to cheer in the realms of scholarship and research.

During the 2010-2011 and 2012-2013 academic years, the University was ranked No. 2 in the nation for Fulbright Scholars. In the new millennium alone, nearly 50 Fulbright grants were awarded to CSU faculty, who lectured and conducted research abroad as part of this prestigious international exchange program. CSU has sent Fulbright Scholars to South America, Europe, Africa, the Middle East and Asia. The invaluable global perspectives that they brought back with them enriched the entire University community.

CSU also was ranked among the top 20 percent of universities in the nation for research and development, according to the National Science Foundation (NSF).

The NSF awarded a $1.5 million grant to Dr. Antonie van den Bogert, Dr. Dan Simon and Dr. Hanz Richter of the Washkewicz College of Engineering for a four-year project to develop a prosthetic leg that emulates able-bodied gait and utilizes a groundbreaking energy-regeneration system. This revolutionary device promised to dramatically improve the quality of life for people with above-knee amputations. The team conducted research in the Parker Hannifin Human Motion and Control Laboratory at CSU, a state-of-the-art facility that opened in 2013, complete with a special treadmill that uses motion sensors and multiple cameras to capture the intricacies of human movement. The lab was created through a $1.5 million endowment from local Fortune 500 company Parker Hannifin, a global leader in motion and control technologies and systems. Parker Hannifin also funded a research fellowship program for CSU graduate students, as well as an undergraduate scholarship program that included internship and co-op opportunities.

Across the University, boundaries of knowledge were being extended in a wide variety of areas by other CSU researchers, including Dr. Taysir Nayfeh (ultraconductive copper wire), Dr. Karla Hamlen (correlations between video gameplay and real-life ethics and problem-solving) and Dr. Peter Bubenik (who developed a new mathematical tool called "the persistence landscape" to facilitate data analysis).

As its 50th anniversary approached, CSU enjoyed a period of unprecedented philanthropic support.

Alumnus Monte Ahuja, whose international auto-transmission supply company Transtar Industries Inc. grew out of an assignment he completed for a CSU marketing course in the 1970s, and his wife, Usha, donated $10 million to the University in 2011. It was the largest gift to date in CSU history, prompting trustees to rename the James Nance College of Business as the Monte Ahuja College of Business.

That same year, the University launched "Radiance: CSU Realizing the Promise," an annual benefit. It has raised more than $2.6 million to provide scholarships for students at risk for dropping out because of financial issues.

In appreciation of Monte and Usha Ahuja's $10 million gift to CSU, the Board of Trustees announced the naming of the Monte Ahuja College of Business. Dr. Berkman, left, welcomed Monte and Usha Ahuja at the college's dedication on September 23, 2011.

Alumnus Don Washkewicz and his wife, Pam, and the Parker Hannifin Foundation announced a $10 million gift to CSU's College of Engineering on November 19, 2013. It was renamed the Washkewicz College of Engineering in recognition of the transformative donation.

In 2013, another outstanding CSU graduate – Don Washkewicz, chairman, CEO and president of Parker Hannifin Corporation – and his wife, Pam, as well as the Parker Hannifin Foundation made a $10 million donation. In honor of their generosity, the Fenn College of Engineering was rechristened the Washkewicz College of Engineering. Simultaneously acknowledging an important link to the past, Stilwell Hall – longtime home of the engineering college – was renamed Fenn Hall.

The following year, a $3.6 million gift from the Jack, Joseph and Morton Mandel Foundation and the Mandel Supporting Foundations enabled CSU to create the University's newest academic division: the Jack, Joseph and Morton Mandel Honors College.

In 2014, the University closed the books on a record-setting year for fundraising, with $20.3 million attained. CSU also reached a five-year high for alumni giving.

The Jack, Joseph and Morton Mandel Foundation and the Mandel Supporting Foundations made a $3.6 million gift on June 4, 2014, to CSU to create the Jack, Joseph and Morton Mandel Honors College. Morton Mandel, right, is pictured with Dr. Berkman.

Through it all, CSU sought to establish itself as a best-in-class urban university, inextricably intertwined with the surrounding community. In his corner office on the top floor of the Parker Hannifin Administration Center, with its panoramic downtown views, Dr. Berkman was fond of telling guests that it was virtually impossible to tell where the campus ended and the rest of Cleveland began – which, of course, was precisely the point for a truly engaged institution of higher education in an urban setting.

In early 2012, the border between the University and the thriving theatre district next door officially blurred when the curtain went up on the Arts Campus at PlayhouseSquare. This unique collaboration among CSU, PlayhouseSquare and Cleveland Play House enabled students to hone their skills alongside arts professionals in the largest performing-arts center outside New York City. A $30 million renovation converted the historic Allen Theatre into versatile performance spaces for CSU's Department of Theatre and Dance, which made its debut on the Allen's main stage with a Bard-goes-Bollywood re-imagining of William Shakespeare's *A Midsummer Night's Dream.*

The Arts Campus also includes the Galleries at CSU, a stylish exhibition space, as well as classrooms, rehearsal spaces and art studios in the Middough Building.

The campus community was invited to a special preview of the new CSU Arts Campus at PlayhouseSquare in the Middough Building, home to CSU's art, dance and theatre programs, on February 24, 2012. Pictured from left are CSU President Emeritus Michael Schwartz, Board of Trustees member June Taylor and Dr. Ronald M. Berkman.

A pair of similarly successful collaborations between CSU and the Cleveland Metropolitan School District (CMSD) further demonstrated the power of partnerships.

Campus International School, which opened in 2010, is an urban public school that set out to deliver an education on par with that offered by private schools. As of the 2014-2015 academic year, it served grades K-6, with a grade level to be added each year until it reached 12th grade. Accredited as an "IB World School" by the International Baccalaureate Organization, the school embraced a rigorous curriculum with an international focus, complete with Mandarin Chinese language instruction for all students. Test scores indicated that Campus International School was a top performer in the region.

The school was bolstered by the resources of the Center for Urban Education at CSU, led by Dr. Justin Perry, who received a $1 million grant from the U.S. Department of Education's Institute of Education Sciences to create the "Making My Future Work" college- and career-readiness program.

Another CSU-CMSD joint venture, MC²STEM High School, found a new home in 2013 in the Rhodes West Building on the University campus. There, 11th graders and 12th graders who were studying science, technology, engineering and math quickly settled into a stimulating academic setting, including renovated classrooms and a state-of-the-art fabrication laboratory. For many MC²STEM students, CSU provided their first up-close exposure to a university campus and opened their eyes to the possibilities of post-secondary education.

For Dr. Berkman, the ultimate goal was to create an "education park" at CSU that would prepare Cleveland students for success in higher education.

In an era of joining forces and thinking big, perhaps the most dynamic collaboration of all found CSU and Northeast Ohio Medical University teaming up to address the unique health-care needs of metropolitan areas, where concerns such as education, housing and income affected lives and access to healthy living. Launched in 2013, the partnership encouraged students from Greater Cleveland to complete undergraduate and postgraduate coursework at CSU, enroll in the College of Medicine at NEOMED to earn a Doctor of Medicine degree and return after residency to work in medically underserved communities in Northeast Ohio.

Top: Campus International School, a partnership between CSU and the Cleveland Metropolitan School District, served students in grades K-2 when it opened in August 2010, with plans to add a grade each year until becoming a K-12 school. In 2014, the school received International Baccalaureate accreditation.

Bottom: Officials from CSU, the Cleveland Metropolitan School District and the KeyBank Foundation celebrated the grand opening of Cleveland's MC²STEM High School on November 18, 2013, in Rhodes Tower West on the CSU campus. The ribbon was cut with a laser – a fitting touch for a school that specializes in science, technology, engineering and math.

For every collaboration that played out on a grand scale, grassroots efforts by the dozen further strengthened the bonds between CSU and its hometown. In January 2014, the Office of Civic Engagement (a new branch of CSU's Division of University Engagement) announced the first recipients of its Civic Engagement Grants, made possible through a gift from the Jack, Joseph and Morton Mandel Foundation. Grants ranging from $2,500 to $5,000 were awarded to faculty members and student organizations to support a range of projects across multiple Cleveland neighborhoods, from literacy tutoring for young students to technology tutoring for senior citizens.

With CSU and Cleveland moving forward together, there was good reason to be guardedly optimistic – a tone that came across loud and clear when Dr. Berkman addressed the City Club of Cleveland on March 28, 2014.

"[T]he university must not be a remote walled city, but rather knitted into the very fabric of the city," Dr. Harold Enarson, CSU's first president, declared when he spoke before the same forum in 1972.

Much had changed at CSU and in Cleveland in the intervening decades, although Dr. Berkman's address at the City Club revisited a familiar refrain: the vital importance of the symbiosis between the University and its hometown.

"The true advantage for our students is the city of Cleveland," said Dr. Berkman, who had received a contract extension the previous year that would keep him at the helm of CSU through 2017.

"Our quest [is] to make the city, with its incredibly rich resources, an extended classroom for our students," he said. "Everything I do [is] with deep intention to better the University and to better the city. I think that will happen synergistically.

"Above all, my paramount intention is to serve our students, to provide them with a best-in-class urban education, to see them through to graduation day and to prepare them not only to succeed in their chosen career, but in all their endeavors."

For CSU and for Cleveland, the next chapter was wide open. First, though, there was a party to throw.

Scenes from Green Turns Gold Weekend, September 2014 (from top left): Huge puppets loomed over the Parade of the Decades; young partygoers especially enjoyed the green and gold confetti; Norris Cole, left, got a chance to catch up with Magnus and CSU Men's Basketball Coach Gary Waters; Mitchell's Ice Cream unveiled its Green Turns Gold flavor in honor of CSU's 50th anniversary; hip-hop violinist Svet kept the Block Party going well after dark; and fireworks capped the unforgettable evening.

"Here, There, Everywhere Vikings!"

CLEVELAND STATE UNIVERSITY CELEBRATES 50 YEARS

People of all ages were on the move again, but this time, they were marching to celebrate Cleveland State University's golden anniversary.

"Here, there, everywhere Vikings!" a beaming CSU President Ronald M. Berkman declared as he surveyed the nearly 5,000-strong crowd of students, alumni, faculty, staff and friends who packed campus for CSU's 50th Anniversary Block Party and Homecoming Parade of the Decades on September 19, 2014. The festivities were part of Green Turns Gold Weekend, which also included the Distinguished Alumni Awards ceremony and other events.

"This is the most incredible show of CSU spirit that I have seen," Dr. Berkman said.

Revelers lined Euclid Avenue for the parade, led by Grand Marshal Norris Cole, the former Vikings basketball standout who went on to win two NBA Championships with the Miami Heat. Marching alongside him through a blizzard of green and gold confetti were honorary Grand Marshals Dr. Berkman and Wally Morton, who coached CSU's swimming and diving teams from 1974 to 2014.

Stepping off from the Student Center Plaza, the parade featured students and graduates spanning a half century of CSU history, including representatives from various student organizations, athletic teams, sororities and fraternities. Their ranks also included musicians, huge puppets and, of course, CSU's mascot: Magnus. They made their way down Euclid to East 18th Street, where DJ Lo-Key, the Avenue band and hip-hop violinist Svet performed on a large stage to keep the party going in front of the Monte Ahuja College of Business.

In honor of the occasion, Mitchell's Ice Cream unveiled its new Green Turns Gold flavor (toasted pistachio ice cream with a ribbon of caramel), which had partygoers standing in a long line for a free sample. Among the other attractions were food trucks, a beer garden and family-friendly activities. At the end of the sun-drenched and unseasonably warm day, the celebration continued with fireworks and late night dancing in the streets – and on the Student Center Plaza.

A proud past had brought Cleveland State University to this point. An unlimited future awaited.

A NOTE FROM THE AUTHOR

It has been my pleasure to spend time researching and writing about the history of my alma mater, Cleveland State University.

I came to CSU in the fall of 1977 as an 18-year-old freshman, having recently graduated from Hawken Upper School in Gates Mills, Ohio. I can remember feeling totally overwhelmed by what seemed to be the incredible size of the campus. Despite the fact that I had a campus map glued to the inside back cover of my spiral notebook, it took a while for me to get my bearings on the long and winding road that would lead from my undergraduate studies to membership on the University's faculty.

Like many CSU students, I always worked at least one job while struggling to juggle the responsibilities associated with family and school. I often imagined that Margaret Walker Alexander understood exactly what that was like when she wrote, "The struggle staggers us." When I consider that struggle today, however, I can't help smiling when I think about some of the individuals who offered encouragement along the way and convinced me that the struggle was worthwhile.

Dr. Butler Jones was my first favorite professor, and he was a brilliant sociologist. I found Dr. Diane Dillard to be an amazing project director, and I always enjoyed working with her to plan the annual Black Aspirations Week activities. Dr. Earl Anderson helped me appreciate the value of co-curricular programming, when we planned and presented the Minority Artist Residency Series in the 1980s. Dr. Anderson's support for my work continued during his tenure as the interim dean of the College of Arts and Sciences.

I will always be indebted to Professor Mareyjoyce Green, who introduced me to the work of the National Women's Studies Association and whose generosity is exceeded only by her humility. Dr. A. Grace Lee Mims, who holds an honorary doctorate from CSU, always encouraged me to find my voice, and she taught me to sing some of the world's most beautiful music, including African American spirituals.

Through it all, my mother, Mrs. Lonzrine Williams, was my rock, my spiritual mentor and the best childcare provider that any college student and working mother could ever hope for. All of the aforementioned individuals – and others too numerous to list in this small space – made a world of difference in my life.

Today, as a 55-year-old grandmother, I am simply amazed at how much our University and downtown Cleveland have changed since 1977. I really love it when so many members of our energetic and incredibly diverse student body point with pride to the fact that they live on campus, or when I see the Great Lakes Science Center and other significant monuments to the waterfront development that Dr. Virginia Benson lectured about in my undergraduate urban studies classes. Most of all, I am truly proud of the fact that I have been a faculty member for more than 20 years, and I have seen some of my former students – including Dr. Ronnie Dunn, associate professor in the Maxine Goodman Levin College of Urban Affairs – go on to become distinguished scholars and educators in their own right.

All told, my CSU experiences add up to one amazing learning journey, and, as the late Maya Angelou said, "I wouldn't take nothing for my journey now!"

All Hail, Alma Mater!
Regennia N. Williams, Ph.D.

Regennia N. Williams, Ph.D., is an associate professor of history at Cleveland State University and founder and director of the Initiative for the Study of Religion and Spirituality in the History of Africa and the Diaspora. She is the founding editor of *The Journal of Traditions and Beliefs* and the co-author of *Through the Lens of Allen E. Cole: A Photographic History of African Americans in Cleveland, Ohio.* She received a Fulbright Fellowship for research and teaching in Ile-Ife, Nigeria, in 2010.